FEEL SO REAL

FEEL SO REAL

TONY JASPER

MarshallPickering
An Imprint of HarperCollins*Publishers*

First published in Great Britain in 1991 by Marshall Pickering

Marshall Pickering is an imprint of
HarperCollinsReligious
Part of HarperCollinsPublishers
77--85 Fulham Palace Road, London W6 8JB

The Author asserts the moral right to be identified
as the author of this work

Typeset by Medcalf Type Ltd, Bicester, Oxon
Printed and bound in Great Britain by
HarperCollinsManufacturing, Glasgow

For Roy and Jill Jones
Inger Rise
Carole Page
Nigel Goodwin

CONTENTS

THE PERHAPSES, MAYBES AND YESSES

Billy Idol may be British, but he enjoys greater popularity in the United States than he does here. However, his is a name most people recognize, and some will recall that he fronted one of punk's more accessible outfits – Generation X.

When Billy was involved in a nasty accident during 1990, it was reported that during his sojourn in hospital he had turned to God. Soon the story was embellished, possibly beyond all recognition, and Idol later spent time denying its truth. Naturally, it would have been a pretty dramatic turn around if one of rock's wild ones were to say that he was a believer. It was not so.

The saga is a good illustration of the care Christians should take in making claims for this, and other purported stories; but that said, it is my definite impression that within the world of contemporary music the Spirit is definitely at work.

I've always advanced the view that the music scene has never been devoid of the spiritual, and indeed would closely align myself to the view of someone like writer Steve Turner who is known in more recent times for his book *Hungry For Heaven* (Virgin). Turner starts with the right question – "What are people religious about today?" – rather than the one that asks, "Are people religious today?"

Steve's basic pivotal statement and assertion says: "A search for transcendence existed behind the best of rock'n'roll, from Elvis Presley and James Brown to U2 and Prince, and this was to be expected because humans are religious by nature.''

In *Strait* magazine, Spring 1990, Turner remarked how some ''secular'' critics thought that the religious instinct was about as significant to rock'n'roll as the instinct to wear dark glasses.

He begged to differ, and so would I. But this book is not concerned to argue the pros and cons of the two stances. Here, quite simply is a pot pourri of testimony that follows the many tracks of music people as they have searched for Christ themselves. For the most part the profiles are of musicians with a Christian perspective, but there is also a lengthy dissertation on what I have called the perhapses and maybes. These are the artists I have met and interviewed, and heard on record, who clearly take the Gospel seriously but who remain uncertain where they might go next, and as yet keep a distance from a definite Christian community. You will find their stories in the final section of the book.

In *Rock Solid* (Word 1986), I described many of the encounters I have had with music stars who have been willing to demonstrate and share their faith. The book's testimony was in striking contrast to the overall message of *Pop Goes The Gospel* by John Blanchard (Evangelical Press), a book that has enjoyed high sales and exerted a major influence. While I would question many of that book's sources, I would not object to some of the strident condemnations it makes of certain areas associated with the pop world. But its basic weakness lies in the author's refusal to accept that religious influence is strong and rife in popular music, and always has been. In my book *Jesus And The Christian In A Pop Culture* (Robert Royce 1985) I listed hundreds of record tracks that have a religious dimension, and in *Rock Solid* there was an impressive list of music people whose lives and music are underwritten by the Gospel. Vital Christian faith can be and is being sustained in popular music, by the people you will meet in this book, and many more.

Since 1985, I have continued to interview music people, go to gigs, hear music, and occasionally travel the road. I am now more than ever conscious that the Gospel is making sense to an increasing number of people. In this sphere the people of Greenbelt have provided a powerful influence. Many music people speak highly of the event, artists such as Deacon Blue, River City People and The Proclaimers. They have been impressed by the company, by the care and love they have been shown. Also the Arts Centre Group, especially its members Dave Berry, Nigel Goodwin and Cliff Richard, is a blessed area in which music people have come into contact with Christian things, for on its premises, music stars have often argued about the nature of faith, sometimes into the early hours of the morning.

So here is a general review of what it is for some people to feel real. It is intended to inform and build up faith. Some of those I have interviewed especially for this book have wanted to use their testimony so that they might encourage others to seek the things of God and Jesus. At times even a hardened rock critic and listener such as myself has felt bowled over by the strong passionate expressions of joy and happiness.

So, read on into the land of perhapses, maybes and yesses!

TONY JASPER

January 1991

1

MICHAEL BEEN

The Call

"There is so much despair in the world. I am I suppose in a glamorous position but I am into expressing what some call old-fashioned things, and at risk of sounding corny in today's times, I am saying life is precious, that people do not have self-esteem."

You arrive at a place where you start to see the bigger picture.

Michael Been wanted a bigger picture of life. But he carried his past in tow. He was raised in Oklahoma City. By the age of seven he was performing the songs of rock'n'roll heroes such as Elvis Presley and Buddy Holly, and at the same time assimilating music from country and western stars like Hank Williams and Patsy Cline, and he was to perform their music on a television show called *Big Red Shingig*. But Oklahoma never provided the right atmosphere for the youthful Michael, and he escaped to Chicago, the blues capital, where he had first heard this style of music.

"I was raised in the South, and Judaeo-Christian imagery and thought were heavily entrenched in me. I remember as a kid when Elvis came out and my teenage sister turned on to him. I listened to his rock'n'roll albums, and then he came out with an album of all gospel songs. And being pretty innocent at the time, I didn't separate them in my mind, so 'Amazing Grace' and 'Jailhouse Rock' were the same thing to me. I look back on that now, and I realize what I was hearing was an expression of passion – whether physical or spiritual.''

Chicago was only a stepping-stone in his musical career and education, for he later travelled to Los Angeles, after an initial spell in Santa Cruz, where he had met the people who would become The Call. Talking of the others, Been says, "We all had offers to do other things, to play with other people. But when the four of us play together, it's better than any one of us and more than the sum of the parts. That's why we do it."

He didn't know of course that by the end of the Eighties, rock legend Peter Gabriel was to hail The Call as the future of American music. Britain's music weekly *Melody Maker* agreed. The American paper *Rolling Stone* called Been one of the most literate lyricists in rock'n'roll today. The *Los Angeles Times* said The Call was able to deliver what U2 only skirts: an integration of spiritual yearning with blues-based grit. MCA Records described their album *Let The Day Begin* as a crafted package that ranged from the driving rock'n'roll of the title cut, and hit single, to the hymn-like gentleness of "Uncovered" as "hewn from the soul, tempered in the heart, and performed from the gut". Been, speaking of his album said, "Lyrically, it's about our attempt to communicate, our attempt to run away from ourselves . . . and others. It's about self-realization, about healing."

Been was already moving on a spiritual plane. Because of his past, his Christian-based awareness, he believed The Call should rise above the ephemeral nature of much pop music, that they should go beyond the usual ambition of music people, of "getting girls, getting rich, getting famous. It's a matter of writing songs about things I feel deeply about. The closer I write to the bones, about my life, the passion comes out naturally."

Michael's consistent aim and practice has attracted more sensible press coverage than that accorded to most in the rock world. More than one writer has expressed the thought that if the singer-songwriter were to lose his rock calling then he would find a ready response on the inspirational speaker's circuit. Writers have not opposed running long and lengthy quotes, such as "We tend to compartmentalize so much that we don't have a relationship with ourselves. We take from our parents. We take from our friends and the people we've met. We take from society. And somewhere we lose ourselves in all of that. We need to build that relationship with ourselves back up."

He told me, "My idea of songwriting is somehow making positive statements. There is so much despair in the world. I am I suppose in a glamorous position but I am into expressing what some call old-fashioned things, and at risk of sounding corny in today's times, I am saying life is precious, that people do not have self-esteem. And yet Christ came poor, yet what he offers is full of possibilities."

That certainly means that Michael and The Call do not chase commerciality in the manner of many pop stars. "We have a rotten ability to say what's commercial. Ninety per cent of what we hear we don't like. So we think, 'Why even try to be like that?' It's like those people are in a different line of work." It is a case of getting to a point where you start to see a bigger picture of life.

He said, "We resolved The Call would never be compromised by commercial considerations. The particular group of people that comprise my immediate circle of friends don't think anything about me. In fact, what I'm doing is a little embarrassing compared to the legitimacy of their work. My best friend is a chaplain of a state penitentiary. So while I'm sitting around talking about the toughness of the rock'n'roll world, or I'm bitching that I haven't sold 100,000 records, he's helping people try to stay alive and sane.''

His uplifting conversation led the *Los Angeles Times* to headline *"The Call: Heavenly Subject, Earthly Range"*, and their writer Mike Boehm to remark how in "live" concert the band deal from a "Christian Everyman perspective, some of the deepest, most thought-provoking issues of religious belief and spirituality. The Call's undogmatic songs are about yearning for connections with the divine, suffering doubts, and finding the hope that allows one to keep on striving for a sense of grace.''

But Mike is aware that anyone who has seen a bigger picture of life, and wishes to say this, can easily be cynically dubbed as a bore, especially in the frenetic, ever-changing and ultimately barren world of pop music.

And he is hesitant about brandishing big slogans for himself. "People start making all kinds of judgements about you. I merely want to affirm the God who has called me, the historical truths about God and man. About a relationship with God who is seen in Jesus. It has meant so much to my life.''

And he told me, "Give me a healthy and not a repressed Christian. So many people keep coming up with their definitions, and I am saying 'their' impositions. There are some people who inflict upon others artificial guilt. And sometimes we are vulnerable to this. The faith inside of you can die, and you find yourself further away from where you should be going.''

Michael believes that there is always a continual fight for truth, and that indeed, on a personal level, there is always a battle against anti-spiritual forces that would preach that life is "living today as though nothing matters tomorrow". He says, "I believe that people have to go back and look at the early philosophies. There must be a mighty spiritual explosion."

And it is in Jesus where there is found the person who presents the bigger picture of life.

2

MAIRE NI BHRAONIAN
"Just Brilliant!"

Clannad

"I felt more content with myself. You know it becomes an enormous relief to know there is Something there, a lovely feeling. I don't know what I did, it just came, just brilliant . . . but it's how I felt and how I feel now; coming to faith has been so marvellous."

The conversation that became infused with spiritual content had started out as a straight interview. Maire is a founder, lead singer and sometimes songwriter of the Irish band Clannad, which is very much a family affair, though slightly less so now than in past times. The band had just released a new album: *Sirius* was the group's first foray into what some have called "LA technology", and for a while we wandered a little inconsequentially through its tracks. The stopping-point of a polite, not unfriendly interview, came with mention of the song "Something to Believe In". I inquired if this suggested that Maire had faith, or was in the process of enquiring and looking for just that — something to believe in.

To my joy and pleasure, Maire told me that her faith, fairly dormant for many years, had been replenished. From that point my phone bill took an uncomfortable lurch upward, as we talked for a long time, and shared our spiritual search and findings. It seemed that we had much that we could give praise for, and that both of us could claim Christ as our Saviour.

The upshot was some more meetings, and in terms of this book a long meeting, and later a phone talk shortly before Christmas 1990.

Much of Maire's present strong faith stems from her relationship with Tim Jarvis, a photographer of skill and sensitivity.

Jarvis found himself dispatched to Ireland by the pop paper *New Musical Express* in place of someone else who couldn't make the trip. He arrived in Dublin knowing little about the Bhraonian family. But he couldn't fail to be enchanted by the west coast of Ireland, and by Maire's undoubted love for Donegal. More, he was fascinated by Maire herself. After returning to Britain, with his photographic assignment completed, he wrote to her and suggested that she might like to have dinner with him the next time she was in London. As it happened, she had to come over a week later. They met. So began a progression from friendship to love and, on January 12 1991, marriage.

For Maire her meeting with Tim, as indeed the way faith has come to her, can only be part of God's plan. Her faith had already become more real before meeting him, but the essential miracle here is that she should fall in love with someone who wasn't originally intended for the session work with Clannad, and that he should be an ardent Christian.

"Donegal is a lovely place, it has a magical beauty. We showed people around, gave them food to eat, and it was a great night. And then he wrote to me. He talked of the wonderful time he had had. He told me – the flatterer – that I was one of the grandest ladies and that he'd love to meet me again.

"It was love at first sight, we had so much to share and find in common. To me, it was all God's, He was bringing this into being. I mean, this was happening to me, to share myself, my love, my faith with someone who could meet me on these levels!"

This experience led her toward the central feeling that permeates her present Christian experience, "I feel that God has something for me, when I thought that in no way could anything like this be for me. And now it seems we've come a long way. I know now that really it is not important that we do such-and-such a job. It is the case of believing that God has something for us, that we should be willing to hear. I feel sure that there is now something else ahead. God has plans. I feel it is so brilliant."

Previous to meeting Tim, Maire had been questioning and searching. She had reached a time in her life when she found herself evaluating exactly where she had reached. In musical terms Clannad had grown from being an Irish folk group that had spent much time on the continent rather than in England, into an international act.

Maire says, "We drew so much from songs and tunes that have been around for hundreds of years and, as for our sound, we never thought of it." Her family had roots that extended back through the centuries of Irish history. The group name, Clannad, is Gaelic for "family", and at the outset, the group was a foursome. "At that point, Pol was singing and playing guitar. I was learning the harp. The band used to practise in my father's bar" (he was a noted Irish band leader, Leo O'Bhraonian). "They had to do eight minutes for this contest and thought they'd do an instrumental. So I said I know a piece – 'Brian Boru's March' on harp; actually, it was the only piece I knew. So all of a sudden, one night at the bar, I was in the band and lead singer as well."

This was in 1976, and from those tentative beginnings, the sudden spotlight of fame came their way when they were asked to score a series for Yorkshire TV. "Harry's Theme" showed Maire's voice in all its stunning beauty. It was a major hit, and the album, *Magical Ring*, which was their debut set for RCA, stayed in the charts for six months.

Later they worked on the songs for the Goldcrest/HTV series, *Robin of Sherwood*, that produced the album *Legend*. Clannad received a British Academy Award for the best soundtrack of the year. They became the first Irish group to win this prestigious award. The following year, in 1986, Maire teamed with Bono from U2 for the big hit single "In a Lifetime".

Macalla, *Sirius*, and *Past Present* (a compilation set) were the ensuing albums before their top ten British hit of 1990, *Anam*. This album received enormous praise and sales response, with acclaim, and units sold far in excess of the previous, more modern-sounding release. But certainly some critics reacted with undue hysterical criticism of *Sirius*, causing Maire to comment, "Some of it was rather over the top, I don't think some people listened very carefully. I think some people looked at the sleeve and saw that some American musicians were involved, and from that they made an assumption before even listening." It seemed Maire and the group had looked for a change: "It gave us the excitement of wondering how it would go to have an American producer and so forth, with our sound, and some said it cut across our perceived fragile sound."

Through some of the musical period that has been described Maire was personally searching and looking. She had become more acutely aware of the emptiness that often accompanies the apparent show-biz froth, or at least, that is how fans often perceive things.

"Obviously, for me, life has changed a lot. I mean, for one thing I had a brilliant childhood, though some would have called it rather sheltered. I had a brilliant youth. Everything, for instance, television, was late in Donegal, and so I was not aware of many things. There was time to grow up. I was a child for a long time! And I felt very protected. I suppose I lived in innocence of the things that so many kids know now, like drugs.''

She speaks of the toll that performing can take, of the many nights on the road, and the come-down emotionally from the "high" of performance. "And you get an awful lot of fawning people, of people hanging around.'' Fortunately she had friends, Bono of U2 being one of them.

"We've spent a lot of time together and we've discussed God and talked about Him, which was great, and it's meant a lot to me on my spiritual journey. Some of our conversation has inspired me. My background is Catholicism, though now I span such a boundary, but it gives me support, it does make you aware of God's presence by its very calendar of events. But it always gave me a feeling that I could only pray through the saints and not to God directly. Bono helped me on the latter path, it was an immense discovery.''

Her gradual coming back home to God gave her a greater relaxation, and "I felt more content with myself. You know it becomes an enormous relief to know there is Something there, a lovely feeling. I don't know what *I* did, it just came, just brilliant, if I am not overdoing the word, but it's how I felt and how I feel now; coming to faith has been so marvellous.''

And as well as the paramount importance of this experience, there came Tim, and the heavens opened for them both, to leave them genuinely amazed and thrilled that they should be part of such a discovery.

Maire had already been married, but things had not

worked out. "I think the wildness, if that is the word, came in my life when that marriage broke up. And again I think I had gone through a long time of behaving like one of the boys, and I was very bold. Now I see that the body is precious. It should be used, sexually, in the overall context of how you view yourself. So with Tim, I was celibate until we married."

And what of drugs? Not surprisingly she admitted that she had been offered cocaine – "Who hasn't in the music business?" – and refused both that and LSD. "I think I had seen the bad things drugs can do, and I was scared it might mean me going mad or something. As a person growing up in Donegal, and for the band, the boys, my brothers and larger family, there's enough lift in the country, the legends, the music, not to need stimulants!"

Maire also spoke of the emotional pressures that result from being away from home, and of being the subject of speculative newspaper reports, both having a direct effect upon a marriage. She accepts she was at fault in her previous marriage. She points out that there is pressure on the other partner who might begin to think his other half is having a whale of a time and he is not, that pictures showing you with another person can be given a wrong interpretation when seen somewhere else in the cold light of day.

Fortunately, there were no children from the first marriage but she has hopes from her new relationship. Faith has given her a new stability, a new awareness, and a new partner, but "Don't think it's been all easy, it takes time to take down the fences."

Perhaps it's because Maire grew up in a large family situation that she has extreme modesty, and this at first can be given a false interpretation. It is not easy to hear someone as famous, as marvellous, speaking with hesitation about her vocal powers. "I am just the way I am, with my limitations. I struggle along. I think it was a bonus that when Tim first met me he knew little, so he took me as he found me, without all the trappings of presumed success."

The new-found faith that has come from the trials and tribulations of the last few years has concrete underpinning. Apart from talking with Bono, she has found a new friend in Maria McKee, once of Lone Justice, who was a number-one-selling artist during 1990, and who now spends a great deal of time in Dublin. In addition, Maire ensures that she keeps in close contact with a Christian community.

"I always go somewhere when I'm travelling, and I make sure my schedule permits it, so that wherever we are, even if on the move, I stop and go to church. There's a beautiful Catholic cathedral in Melbourne, and in Christchurch, New Zealand, an Anglican cathedral, I remember vividly. I was welcomed in both. And with those two, and elsewhere, I have been so encouraged. People have been so welcoming into God's house.

"So I determine to find a place where I can be in fellowship. You have to work at it, you have to arrange it. But it's important that I do so. I've always carried a prayer book with me, and I've always thrown it into my suitcase, but to be with God's people, that is good. It is that special thing. I do need something. I do need spiritual sustenance. Obviously now, with Tim, there is much time for prayer and we can read and discuss the Bible together. We discuss it a great deal."

Maire cannot quite get over the simple fact that someone so close to her shares her faith. "I mean that I should be able to begin and end the day with someone I can pray with – Oh, we have started reading so many things together — and that we are travelling in the same direction. It all seems just right and I praise God. We read a bit, talk a bit, pray a bit!''

So now she has very much what she has looked for. Into the frenetic world of self, the music world, the haste and bustle of its commercialism, there has come this deep peace of God, in worship and prayer, and also in a life's partner for the future. Now she feels that the right things are being done, the right things are being said, and that underwriting all is prayer, this close contact with the God who created, who came in Jesus, and is found now, today and every day.

But what word, phrase or sentence can summarize all this? In itself this is somewhat of a tall order, but Maire has said several times, "God has something for us." Something for Maire, for Tim, and also for each of us.

Say it loudly — "God has something for me."

3

JOCELYN BROWN

"I got the power"

"This was what I wanted to be – possessed with his power. I shouted Amen and I shouted Amen! I know now I can't function without knowing this. But why me? I am the least of the deserving, yet He had laid His hands upon me. Amen!"

It was "moving house" time for Jocelyn Brown but she had a few moments to talk some more about her faith. We had met several months before, not long after her exciting voice had helped to catapult Snap to the top of the charts all over the world with "The Power". And soon after that she had a big British dance floor hit, "Freedom", a number she had penned with her daughter Kai Shaw.

Central to her testimony is the cry that has been offered by believers down the ages, "How can I have deserved such love? It has made me happy, so happy, and sometimes it overwhelms me."

We talked of her early days. She stressed the importance of "roots", and how these early formative experiences never go away. She had grown up in North Carolina, and her first church experience was in the local Baptist church. The family moved home, and set up in New York. For a while she savoured many kinds of religious expression, from Catholicism to Methodism, for she had family in the Methodist way.

Jocelyn was impressed but not smitten by what she

heard and saw. She was hungry for greater power; she had read and wanted to know more about the Spirit.

One Sunday, she wandered into a Pentecostal church, and even though she was well versed in black gospel worship with its high degree of drama and emotion, she had to agree that this place was resounding with praise in a wonderful way. "I think I found the 'new' in powerful prayer, in prophecy, in straight teaching on right and wrong. And there was dedication. I began the path of realizing that I wasn't really saved. I knew the great statements, but I wanted my own testimony."

A time of knowing, of being "persuaded", as the old preachers used to say, was to come: she attended faithfully and heard more of the Christ who had died for her. But once more the family was on the move, this time to the American capital, Washington DC.

She was sixteen, and it was the early Sixties. Her uncle had a church in the city, and she began attending it. She found it even more powerful than the "fire-baptized" churches of New York and the South. It was deeper, and as she put it, "They get to it." She loved the teaching, and she identified closely with the message. She knew now that she must dedicate herself; she felt herself touched all over by the Spirit, "It was SUCH an experience, SUCH impact. This was what I wanted to be – possessed with His power. I shouted Amen and I shouted Amen! I know now I can't function without knowing this. But why me? I am the least of the deserving, yet He had laid His hands upon me. Amen!"

She talks of her experience as something that she couldn't run from. "Once it's there, it's part of you. I just accepted Him there and then. I know He died and rose for me, and He gave me the second chance. I just hadn't really allowed Him into my life. I hadn't allowed the Spirit to take control I asked Him to bless me, and He did. I found this goodness and this love. That moment was a gift to be treasured as long as I live.''

Once in flow, Jocelyn rages onward! For her, faith springs from the impossible, and the ''impossible'' rests in the fact that God so loved us that He died for us – and here she joins with so many, with the ordinary and the great, and assuredly with Charles Wesley who wrote in his famous hymn, ''And can it be'':

Amazing love! – how can it be
That Thou, my God, shouldst die for me!

''That's right,'' says Jocelyn, and for a moment we share our common joy. ''He will keep me,'' she adds, and then stresses the importance of responding, and not letting time march on without commitment, of moments and experiences that may be missed.

She talks of God having found a way for her, of having blessed her by giving her a voice that has power and authority. ''I didn't know I had this. I was in an all-girl choir in Washington, laid-back, not making an impact.'' Soon she realized that she had the power and presence ''to be out there'' on stage, filling an auditorium with the sound of her voice. ''When you know you have a gift, then you must appreciate it. And you must do that each and every day. I have had so many stirring moments.''

She talks of being so grateful, she talks of wonder, she talks of praise, of God's love. ''Man is one part, God is the Lord of all. He has made a way for me. I can say that I know Him, and I acknowledge His power.''

Of course, life hasn't run on this high level constantly, but she is deeply conscious of his Spirit being there, and sometimes, at moments, when sharing her convictions with another, everything comes to the surface in a seemingly overwhelming tidal wave of praise, and she has to speak with what might seem, to the more restrained, extravagant language.

She has shared her faith with other singers and musicians. She speaks with pleasure about working with Andrae Crouch, and recalls a meeting with mega-star Michael Jackson: "He's a wonderful boy, and likes to laugh a lot. You know you read so many things about him but I only know what I brought back from meeting him, and that was of a great person."

Indeed, this was the impression gained by Andrae Crouch when he met Michael, and I recall Andrae telling me in Kragero, Norway, that Michael was a very spiritual person. And Jocelyn concurs. Both report, from separate meetings and work with Michael, that it may well be that he has left the Jehovah Witness faith, and really found true belief.

Jocelyn had some more removals waiting for packaging, and the conversation between us had to end. I came away filled with an awareness of her vitality and energy, the central power of her existence, and feeling that here was someone who had felt the Spirit's power and who daily marvels that Jesus died for her.

She has The Power.

4

BRUCE COCKBURN

"Let me be a little of your breath."

"He has been totally given to the thought that Christ is found in everyday events . . . He sees God's love tying this world to the next."

For Canadian singer-songwriter Bruce Cockburn, there has been a constant, though intermittent, experience of the presence of Christ.

He was first conscious of this presence when he married. His girlfriend Kitty had persuaded him that their marriage should take place in church. He remembers standing at the altar with Kitty and being conscious of "another" that he assumed must be Christ. He hesitates to describe the event in Damascus Road terms, yet something very definite happened to him. He had met a positive and good "presence". It was the turning point in his whole consideration of the Christian faith, the moment that pushed him into saying "yes" to God, the moment from which he described himself as a Christian, the moment he felt he would take communion.

This has been his most graphic experience of God's presence. There have been other less definable moments, all of which when added together in the sum of his life's journey have become fairly substantial.

Yet it must be said that his Christian life has been sharply divided between the reflective note of his albums of the Seventies where there is often a sureness, and those of the following decade in which he seems acutely conscious of God moving away; but then did not the witer of old ask with pained expression: "Is there any Word from the Lord?" So it is, for instance, that Bruce says in the song "Lily of the Midnight Sky",

> In the rising day
> you keep fading away

but always present has been the desire that he states so simply in "Hills of Morning":

> Let me be a little of your breath
> moving over the face of the deep
> I want to be a particle of your light
> flowing over the hills of morning

for whatever his sense of presence, he has been totally given to the thought that Christ is found in everyday events. The good creation has been distorted, yet it has been rescued, restored and given new life in Jesus.

Bruce Cockburn has been making albums ever since his self-titled set in 1970, and new releases have followed year after year. For many his is the supreme Christian commentary on culture and political-social events in the general record world, yet in spite of his obvious talent his is a voice and prophecy that largely goes ignored. In Britain his work has best been popularized by the Greenbelt Festival organizers, and those responsible for the associated magazine *Strait*. Along with Peter Case, John Hiatt and T-Bone Burnett, he brings a Christian influence to bear at the more intellectual and sophisticated end of the music market.

His faith has had severe testing, and with the major events that have affected his life, his perceptions of the essential nature of the Gospel have undergone change.

In the first place his marriage did not last. The

breakdown caused considerable pain. It meant a severe re-examination of the simplicities of faith that he had carried on board. It is patently untrue to assume that a marriage between people who are both journeying in faith can always hold, through thick and thin. But, like many others, Bruce took it for granted that all would be well.

One major upshot of the dissolution of his marriage was a newly acquired freedom. He accepted an invitation from Oxfam to visit Central America and assess the social and political situation there. The experience hit him hard. He saw human tragedy, and much of it, to his mind, was caused by the policies enacted by the government of the USA. Such an assessment made him no friends among the right wing of the American Moral Majority, and his feelings on this are mirrored powerfully in the song "Gospel of Bondage", found on the 1989 album *Big Circumstance*.

It made him see God's presence in the downtrodden and mistreated. It made him realize that real faith cannot exist in a vacuum, nor can faith reflect or be swallowed up by prevailing national dispositions; faith is never an extension of any government.

Central America has not been his only preoccupation. It has never been forgotten, but, he has since shown concern for the plight of Tibetan refugees, anguished with those who suffered in the aftermath of Chernobyl, and had time to feel and observe city life in the West. Many of his thoughts on these can be found on the *Big Circumstance* album set.

His album issued at the end of the Eighties saw him more overtly spiritual than in some material of that decade. And biblical allusion was precise and clear on a track such as "Shipwrecked at the Stable Door", where the opening words are culled from the Beatitudes. His imagery, too, is vivid. His sense of Presence has led him into more closely aligning this world and the next. The same album has a song entitled "Gift" in which he sees God's love tying this world to the next.

More and more Cockburn has been gripped by this powerful burning love. It is a love that he sees uppermost in his desire to raise the mundane level of existence for all peoples, whether the poor or the affluent citizen wrapped up too snugly in consumerism and so unaware and uncaring about questions of eternity. His musical work, apart from painting vivid pictures of man's fallen nature, provides the call that people should "feel so real".

The Presence felt once so powerfully gains extension in the way in which he sees his role. He is first and foremost an artist, and then comes what he wishes to say. It is not that he is advocating hype and image before content, rather he is concerned that so many people lose their message through inadequate presentation.

But what of his sense of Gods silence? Is that a negative voice? On his album *Big Circumstance* he sings:

Sometimes you can hear the Spirit whispering to you,
but if God stays silent, what else can you do,
just listen to the silence and you will surely see
that God won't be reduced to an ideology
as your gospel of bondage . . .

He has issued nearly twenty albums since 1970. They provide a rich statement of Christian perception. He has translated the various experiences of his life into the poetry and music of song. He has said that his role as an artist lies in reflecting everyone's experience through the artist's experience.

There lies his spiritual honesty. Anyone who wants to know what can lie behind this book's title *Feel so Real* can hardly better their search in contemporary rock music than exploring this theme with Cockburn's songs. It is a pity that some of the angry shouts against rock culture ignore one of the most salient "Christian" voices within its output.

5

ANDRAE CROUCH

"I'm gonna keep on singing."

"I praise the Lord anywhere. Any time. I have one question when I write a new song — 'Does it reach you?' I feel the feedback from an audience if the song is working. I know what is real."

Kragero, Norway, mid-summer 1990, backstage at the eighth Skjaergardsgospel Festival. There is a sudden flurry of movement and anticipation, for the man from America has arrived. Here is Andrae Crouch, gospel singer and songwriter of a special kind, respected outside religious circles for his musical input and performance skills in the world of soul music. He arrives with chattering, smiling friends, he is beaming widely, and obviously glad to renew his long-standing friendship with Norwegian Christians.

Andrae has been many times to Norway, and while he is most welcome as a performing artist, it is as a songwriter that he is regarded with particular respect and affection. On stage during the Festival is the exciting Oslo Gospel Choir, under the conductor, a Methodist, by the name of Tore Aas. And they sing many of his songs. On occasions, the American sings with them, at other times he stands either in front of, or at the side of the actual stage, his mouth often wide open in amazement that a Choir can so splendidly sing his music. At other moments he gurgles like a child with an extra-special present.

Once he was slim, now he is overweight. The facial features have broadened, yet he still bounces and buzzes around, as though he was back in the Sixties, a career and commitment to the Lord just beginning.

Andrae, his fine singing sister Sandra, and older brother Benjamin junior, were born and raised in south Los Angeles, where their parents ran a dry cleaning business. Evenings and weekends, his father exercised an open-air preaching ministry, and also regularly visited a penitentiary. Even at the age of three, Andrae would accompany him. The parents prayed for their children each and every day. This is not in itself a remarkable event for many do, but Andrae remembers it, and believes that it was a formative influence upon his life. He says, "Oh, it's just beautiful to be reared in a Christian home, and to have those memories."

A piano and a gift for music were ever-present realities almost from the time his hands could reach the notes, and his feet the piano pedals. No formal musical education has been his, yet he can play complicated rhythms in any key all over the keyboard, with eyes closed or open. Mention this to the Andrae of the Nineties, and he seems amused, but he would place his thanks in the context of his faith. "What I know — I just learnt it up along the way, God just made it in me." It seems that one day the church people set him down on the piano stool and he just started playing. His first two-handed effort was the Hymn "What a Friend we have in Jesus". He says, "I said to myself that the Lord had given me the gift of music and I should use it to praise Him, and tell His message."

At first his own voice was under-used. He became a choir director of the Los Angeles Teen Challenge Centre. But he began to sing locally with two friends, and Andrae Crouch and the Disciples came into existence. *Take The Message Everywhere*, their first album, was released in 1969.

Since then there have been countless albums, and song compositions. Many of the compositions have come from his own experience, the positive side always emphasized. With disarming simplicity he describes his spiritual walk with his Lord: "He just gives me the songs."

Paul Davis, gospel music writer and historian, recalls how Andrae told him of an occasion when he and others were playing at a convention in San Francisco. "The chords came to me for Psalm 103, 'Bless the Lord, O my soul'. I found a piano down the hall and a group gathered around. We were blessed just singing 'Bless the Lord, O my soul'. Then it totally left me! It was about three months later when we were back for another convention there in the same hotel that it popped up again. So, I sang it and everybody learned it. It's just amazing how the Lord gives a song." At a future date, he recorded the song that was to provide such uplift to Christians of all ages.

I mention this story to Andrae, as we sit and talk in Kragero. "Oh yeah," he says, eyes bulging, "that's right, the Lord is so good." He makes the point that he is forever telling people to do just that: "I don't want them praising me. Everything I am or ever hope to be is of the Lord. Everything!"

Over the years his music has widened. He doesn't stay within the Gospel field, although it is never far away. He has heard many kinds of music and befriended many stars from many genres.

At times his music has been described as a unique fusion of rhythm'n'blues, country, jazz and even Latin rock. Says Andrae, "I wanted these influences to infect me. I sometimes get criticisms from some blacks. I ignore this. I don't believe that if a Gospel group goes to Las Vegas to work, they've sold out, gone slick. I praise the Lord anywhere. Any time. I have one question when I write a new song – 'Does it reach you?' I feel the feedback from an audience if the song is working. I know what is real.''

Hard to pin down in terms of music and audience, Andrae is insatiably a "born again" enthusiast, forever jumping up and down to irresistible rhythms. But times have not always been kind to Andrae. There have been several bouts of bad health, including one such time early in his life when he had a rare type of illness with no known cure. He remembers his mother saying, "I've got confidence God is gonna see you through", and "God did heal me." From that experience and memory he was to write the song "Take a Little Time" (to thank the Lord) that would appear on an award winning album *Keep On Singin'*.

Whatever the case, to use the title of one of his songs, "I'm Gonna Keep on Singing", and he ploughs onward. And more and more these days he takes his faith in song into social and political arenas. Back in America, he runs a twenty-eight-acre ranch, as part of his overall specialized street ministry to lost young people, especially those on drugs. "It's why I do not sing so much professionally. I choose where my heart goes, and it's mostly with these kids."

"I marvel at this gift God has given me," he muses, in an aside, during a conversation about his work amongst unwanted young people. "It's meant as an energy place, a place where 'big' thoughts can start again, but that takes time. I just enjoy this ministry so much. People have to be given new opportunities. But every now and then, I get out the songs, and I travel."

He doesn't pretend things are easy, and he is aware of opposition, for when it comes down to it, not everyone, in spite of pious words and promises, really wants the essential face-to-face contact with the lost. "I guess we set up what we are doing because we wanted freedom from church boards and committees. So it has meant a greater weight on my shoulders, but the Lord gives me strength, and he does so daily, and I praise His name!''

For Andrae, it's always the case of "I'm gonna keep on singing".

6

JESSY DIXON

"You bring the sun out."

"In the past I nearly got burned, it seemed so good that I was there with the stars, on the same platform, and I was getting all this notice. But I had to ask myself what it was that I was believing."

Jessy Dixon and his Singers found favour in the early part of the Seventies with the American Paul Simon. They sang at the famous man's concerts, they joined with him on disc, and Jessy acted and sang in the feature film that starred Paul, *One Trick Pony*.

As a result Jessy became the "flavour of the month" as he lent back-ups on a host of recordings from some of the famous people of the day.

The song *par excellence* of his set was "Jesus is the Answer". He sang it with verve and emotion. People were visibly moved by both his projection and the song's power. Yet amazingly, Jessy lacked the real personal conviction of the faith towards which his song led others. He went through the motions. He did not know Jesus as his personal Saviour.

He spent years singing gospel with Christians before he actually believed in what he was doing. Yet he had had a Christian upbringing. His mother was of the "Sanctified" church, his father a Methodist. He had played and sung in church from an early age. At one time he had gone to music college, but part way through his training he had been whisked away from all that by the famous American gospel music man James Cleveland.

Jessy played piano for James Cleveland and he also sang a little; and with him in Cleveland's musical set-up was organist Billy Preston, who was to find world rock recognition and, more important, know Christ.

Much of Jessy's career is for the gospel musicologist, but suffice it to say that he was much influenced by his work in the Chicago Community Choir. This band of singers visited hospitals and jails, doing it for nothing. Jessy caught something of the Gospel as he saw lives changed and people praising God.

Jessy's upbringing in gospel and in the church, together with his considerable musical skills, meant that he could simulate the right fervour without much strain. Yet at the same time, there was this increasing awareness that maybe there was something in what he was singing about, something that he, of all persons, should find, for his life lacked inner peace and meaning.

So it was that he found and came to know Christ. It happened – just happened. He was suddenly aware. He knew Jesus had died for him. But he was aware that this was only the beginning.

When I met Jessy, along with Andrae Crouch, at the Kragero Gospel Festival in 1990, it was this aspect of his life that he particularly wanted me to stress. He said there were many stories of conversion, but that often in their telling no one emphasized the journey that must be made.

At the time of our meeting Jessy had a new album out, entitled *I Know what Prayer Can Do*, and he told me, "That is the real story, it's no good living without it. It's no good saying, 'It'll be all right, I believe.' Prayer is essential."

Jessy spoke of his deep feeling that people had been praying for him, once they were aware that in times past he had lacked real personal commitment. And he had been conscious of the power of their prayers. "In the music world, it can be hard, and faith can be hard."

The result of their prayer was obvious. "I have become so much stronger as a Christian. In the past I nearly got burned, it seemed so good that I was there with the stars, on the same platform, and I was getting all this notice. But I had to ask myself what it was that I was believing. And, I found the Gospel, and I found it was exciting."

Jessy is a smart dresser. He stood out amongst the more usual festival clothing of denim and denims. He comes cream-suited, very cool. He says he got his dress sense from following the famous soul, R & B and gospel singer Sam Cooke, resolving to dress immaculately. That style, and an overall professional ease that exudes from his set, has made some people uncomfortable. Artists, producers and technicians marvel at an artist who can just stroll into a studio or on stage and deliver, but often audiences are suspicious. To them, the Dixon air of invincibility can seem rehearsed, the process of going through a format.

For Jessy, this is putting him back into his pre-conversion days. "I have to take the criticism and I have to keep going, and I know where I stand. Sometimes you have to stand up against criticism, but I make no bones about what I believe. I am doing more and more concerts and at these, people do give their hearts to Christ. Mahalia Jackson once said to me, 'If you've got something to say, Jessy, then sing it.' And I do."

Meeting someone is not the same as hearing them from a distance. Personally, I found him friendly, and more genuine. If others think otherwise, then that is up to them.

As he sings of Jesus — "You bring the sun out".

7

BOB DYLAN

"Changed my way of thinking."

"What's the Son of God? What does it all mean — dying for my sins?" And he began to accept that this Jesus is real, "and I wanted that."

At the beginning of the 1980s, Bob Dylan became a Christian. He clarified his position with the *Los Angeles Times* music critic Robert Hilburn.

Not really given to religious terms, he admitted to Hilburn that "I truly had a born-again experience." Many were stunned by the news. It was hardly fashionable then for a rock star, much less the most influential male artist in rock history, to admit to such an experience. But no one familiar with his massive catalogue of almost entirely successful albums, and hence his songs, could surely suggest that his conversion came from nowhere.

Apart from the more obvious fact that Dylan, alias Robert Allan Zimmerman, born 24th May 1941, who had his bar-mitzvah on 22nd May 1954, had grown up in a Jewish environment, there was plenty of evidence on his albums that he was a man of acute religious sensitivity. In the merging of the two decades of the Sixties and Seventies, he had produced two of the most eloquent and stirring albums with a powerful religious base, namely *John Wesley Harding* and *New Morning*. And throughout his career his albums had carried religious allusions.

But as a Jew, he had never either accepted Jesus as the true Messiah, foretold in Old Testament prophecies, or seen a particular significance for himself in Jesus' death.

"I had always read the Bible but I only looked at it as literature. I always knew there was a God or a creator of the universe and a creator of the mountains and the sea and all that kind of thing" (hear his "Father of Light" on the album *New Morning*), "but I wasn't conscious of Jesus, and what that had to do with the supreme creator."

So he asked the kind of questions that Christian enquirers have always posed: "What's the Son of God? What does it all mean – dying for my sins?" And he began to accept that this Jesus is real, "and I wanted that." Other sources, especially writer Dan Wooding, talk of his attending the Vineyard School of Discipleship for a five-days-a-week, three-and-a-half month course that brought him into contact with mainstream Christian teaching.

The immediate effect was seen in his recorded work. His first two albums were pure gospel and spiritual. Later he would veer away somewhat from the blanket approach but to this day he never forgoes the inclusion of one or more songs with a Christian emphasis among his general selection of material.

Just as when Cliff Richard made his "Christian pronouncement" there were those who forecast the artist's demise. But only the most anti-Christian, musically-biased person, could suggest that his first post-Christian vinyl assault, *Slow Train Coming*, was anything other than a masterpiece from a musical genius in the rock genre. It was a severe rebuke to those who amazingly conceived that an artist of his stature and awareness would produce a flimsy piece of fundamentalist candy floss.

It was an awesome illustration of his powers. He was imbued with a new philosophy that realized itself in verbal firing on a par with his best days. He produced deadly summaries of society, and of humankind without God and

Jesus. He could be moving, powerfully so in "I Believe in You", matter-of-factly in "Gotta Serve Somebody", humourously in the childlike "Man Gave Names to All the Animals", catching blues and saying it like he felt on "Changed my Way of Thinking" – and there was also the thrill of the big ending which imbued Jewish Messianic prophecies with the Christian teaching on the Second Coming, in "When He Returns".

But in his first musical attempts to express his Christianity Dylan lacked one essential thing; this was love. The music was very much without joy, or shall we say without the essential nature of John 3:16. He was asking for decision, whether a person was for or against Jesus. He saw this as a matter of urgency. He saw dark days ahead, and he spoke of judgement.

It was strange hearing *Slow Train Coming* and then remembering a cutting in my collection that came from a Christian-based magazine that had been published in 1978, in which the writer had seen him as once the central figure in the protest movement but who had now surrendered his dreams and idealism for hedonism and lust. It was seeing Dylan falling below the line of despair (as Francis Schaeffer has put it) and searching for a definitive experience far, far away from the God of the biblical tradition.

Outside the Christian camp there were those such as Mick Farren who thought it unfortunate that the man who was the guru of a generation could become a post-McLuhan hermit.

Since those first heady days, Dylan has ever remained a completely unpredictable character, as some close events in the early Eighties showed. There was association with an ultra-Orthodox Jewish sect, and he returned once more to Jerusalem (he had gone there in 1971, to the Wailing

Wall, wearing a yarmulka, searching, it was said, for his "Jewish identity") to celebrate his son's bar mitzvah. He was a father of five (one of whom was an adopted daughter from his ex-wife Sara), and varied his travels between properties he owned. In an interview he gave to the American journal *Rolling Stone*, he maintained that he accepted both Old and New Testaments as valid, said he got on well with both Orthodox Jew and Christian, and professed belief in an after-life. He did believe "the end" would come, but did not expect it imminently. He expressed sorrow that some major rock stars had wasted their lives, centering on Janis Joplin and Jimi Hendrix.

But it hardly matched up to some of the exultant "Christian" cries of those first days, as very clearly evidenced in some words in an alternative American Christian magazine of the late Seventies: "dance in the street, all you middle-aged flower children – Bobby's home!"

Yet the experience of Jesus lives on, however blurred it may seem at times. Anyone who has heard him in more recent times sing a powerful song, as "In the Garden", can hardly doubt that Jesus is still real for this exceptional artist. In some ways it is miraculous that he has survived with anything left, considering the extraordinary barrage of criticism that came his way in early times from many of his rock followers. And somehow he avoided the pressures from the stronger side of the Christian camp who saw him as the ideal exhibition piece for audiences they hadn't a chance of reaching.

This has been no offering to the library of Dylan critiques. It is far too brief, for a start. My intention has been briefly to centre on the time and moment when to "feel so real" was for Dylan a "Christian" moment. It is a sketchy ending that has followed. But in my defence,

I might also posit the simple point that Dylan rarely talks to anyone outside his own immediate circle. The one sure thing to emerge from all this is equally simple, though profound in implication; no person cannot be changed, and greatness has nothing whatsoever to do with being claimed by Christ.

8

STEVE FAIRNIE and BEV SAGE

"We just are."

"I think we set out to say that as a Christian you can have fun, and can have a good time, that there is a party and there is a carnival. Too often Christians celebrate being safe, and what is that?"

Given their "arty" background, it is no surprise that Steve Fairnie and Bev Sage, under their own names, but also, and sometimes with an assorted cast, under such names as Writz, Famous Names and The Technos, often appear as a couple determined to shock and stun those of conservative and unambitious expression.

Bev has a background in teaching and drama, while Steve studied at the Royal College of Art, London. Their overall interests and skills go beyond their student disciplines. Bev loves fashion, make-up, hand tinted photos, old movies, blue light and light-emitting diodes. She presents television shows, and finds time to raise children. Steve has interests and skills in sculpture, painting, photography and comedy work. He writes advertisement scripts and has graced a few films. Also he adores getting up as a Chaplin look-alike, while Bev is a very passable Marilyn Monroe.

Writz was born at the end of the 1970s, as an outfit daring to stitch up the tatters and tears of punk. The music came accompanied by unusual make-up, masks, old movies, eccentrics and exhibitionists. For a while they became one of the hottest club bands, but then in 1979 the company to which they were signed – Electric Records – went bankrupt. So too did Writz, and they consequently split up.

By rights, at least in terms of creativity and skill, they should be gobbling up the likes of New Kids On The Block, but then show-biz success stories do not always relate to talent. It must be said that the duo have never entertained thoughts of fame and the consequent demands. So, how do they see themselves?

Steve says, "To me, it's about getting up in the morning, and having a bunch of ideas. You know, I've got this affection for the arts. I relish what I do. I'm a happy man." Of him, Bev says disarmingly, "How long have I been married to him? It must be fourteen years. I still don't know him. He keeps on being interesting. In a way he is a simple person, and yet he can be so confusing. He has so many thoughts."

It should not in any way be thought that Mr Fairnie has the monopoly in this relationship when it comes to the unusual. Bev can play a variety of roles, and can perfectly complement his unexpected meanderings. She provides an excellent doubling-up of his visual expressions. He says, "Rather than being soul-searching songwriters we start with a visual, and then write accordingly. We present a concept. To us, that is where it's at. One of our troubles, though, lies with an unfortunate skill of just being ahead of the big commercial break!"

It was at 6.30 a.m. on the fourth of July that Famous Names was born. Seemingly it arose from Steve spending the previous Christmas in hospital with an ulcer. As a result of this he retreated to Nice in the south of France to convalesce. There, his brain developed an overdrive capacity with the result that he thought extra grand, and with Bev put together Writz plus.

In September 1980, Famous Names took off under the mantle of The Circus Tour, which had not just music but a fire-eater, lady wrestlers, a mime and dance troupe, and a support band. They certainly attracted media attention, and there was an especially warm response in Germany. However, good luck and fortune was not theirs. In December 1980, Steve had more trouble with his duodenal ulcer and was rushed into hospital, and the tour was cancelled. He emerged somewhat slimmed down to seven stone and with a waist, envied by many girl fans, of twenty-two inches. Famous Names was to be the first rock show to tour Israel. But financial problems appeared yet again and another split came.

Later Bev and Steve were able to strike out with a recording of their own, *Falling In Love Again*, and The Technos Twins were born for the credits. Several albums followed. Today they still record, have their songs covered by other, more well-known artists, design record sleeves, and indulge in the numerous activities that have been mentioned earlier in this chapter.

But how does all this impinge upon, or at least, relate to their "out front" declaration that they are Christians? "We're a Christian couple making a living. And we like to think that *living* stems from creativity. We do enjoy the church we attend."

Steve originally came from the charismatic fold, while Bev has a Baptist background. Her father is a minister and from early times she sang songs of faith. "I was exposed to it all, 'life, resurrection, life after death, blood, fire, water, the elements,' you name it! I do remember singing the great hymns, powerful potent moments."

This "mix" has resulted in an unexpected Christian expression. For it might be thought that they would go in for some "hard" religious selling. To do this, though, would negate their whole stance as "artists", for they see their role as lying firmly within an artistic tradition. Bev says, "It's like having a passion for paint and light, we sketch in visual forms, embellish in music." Steve sees their work as having the aim of provoking and arresting people into asking the basic questions about life.

He goes the way of the Gospels. "In the New Testament there is teaching on rebirth. We wish to take areas, and explode them with ideas, so that there are signposts for people to see how they could be translating themselves into a new existence. In our society, drugs is one way for some people in a search for rebirth, but we think that leads to even greater restriction."

What grates with Steve is the unwillingness of many to see that there are numerous ways and means of, for instance, giving flesh and blood to a theme such as "new birth", and it is not something that can be simply explained by a few favourite words and phrases, especially when most of these mean nothing to an outsider to Christian faith.

In terms of where he and Bev have worked and their various group incarnations, he says, "I think we left behind a good trail. We went for it, unafraid, and I think we helped people to faith and a sense of being free. Many of those with us in our projects have remained Christians. I think we set out to say that as a Christian you can have fun, and you can have a good time, that there is a party and there is a carnival. Too often Christians celebrate being safe, and what is that?"

Both would wish to make plain that when it comes to essentials they are straight down-the-middle believers, that they are not in the business of picking and choosing what may or may not suit their tastes when it comes to accepted truths. That said, they are not disturbed if they should upset some fellow Christian brothers and sisters.

It is not that there is deliberate intent to sow confusion, misunderstanding or uncertainty. Far from it. "People have got to realize that we work out there in the clubs, and not in churches. And there is a vast difference. And we've never wanted to venture into the safe pastures of singing pleasant religious songs. To us there is no issue in discussing whether a Christian should be making art in a particular place. We know we've never ventured off the whole faith."

And in their work they wish to leave something that will have stirred people, hoping that their songs and sketches will be remembered, and the intent chewed over.

"Look", they say, "we just are." And what is wrong with that? If only more of us could have the Gospel freedom instead of being locked into umpteen negatives that stifle our own growth through the gifts God has given us. After all, we were created TO BE, RIGHT NOW.

9

BOB GELDOF

"Either you do or you don't."

"I don't know when people talk about God or no God, about God and famine, and starving, and suffering, but I know man is killing hundreds of millions of people."

I would not quarrel with the assertion that it is slightly odd, albeit quirky, that Bob Geldof is included in this book. In no way does he claim "Christian" labelling.

I can imagine that there are those who wish Geldof would recover some of his early and more overtly noticeable religious roots, that he might advocate a particular religious stance. So why Geldof? The simple reply is, "And why not?" Hardly an answer, but useful.

In fact there is no cogent reason, other than that he is someone who has followed the essential gospel precept, whereas many who have words and theologies, and occupy time and space with seminars and discussions, cannot obey Jesus' simplicity, to serve and do.

And, yes, I have met him on a number of occasions, the first time now far back into music history, when Geldof and his Boomtown Rats, originally The Nightlife Thugs, issued in the UK the single "Looking After No. 1". Here, it almost made the top ten. At first sight, the words sounded like a useful descriptive few moments on the make-up of many successful British people, but meeting Geldof gave me the realization that it was a mild send-up, occasioned by his past memories of squalor; after all Geldof had joined the organizers of a Dublin soup kitchen in their effort to give sustenance to the down and outs.

And then later talk centred around other hits from the Rats, such as "She's So Modern", "Like Clockwork" (the first top tenner in the UK), and right at the end of the Seventies, "I Don't Like Mondays". This last centred around the Californian schoolgirl Brenda Spencer who shot and killed several schoolmates.

In November 1990, Geldof told me, "People think I had some kind of social conscience in the mid-Eighties, they're wrong. For why? I've always been into people, they've always interested me, intrigued me. OK, I do have that Christian thing of 'doing', and I want people to find purpose for themselves."

Something went wrong for Geldof and the band half-way through 1982 when "Charmed Lives" became the first single to miss the chart. And even if he did have a starring role in *The Wall*, the movie based on Pink Floyd's album of the same title, things went badly awry on the record front, and the last Boomtown Rats UK hit single, "Drag me Down", finished no further than the rather limiting position, 50. It was the decline of the Rats that led some to say that his mid-Eighties Band Aid saga was partly inspired by the desire to resurrect his career; but such a view seems facile. Quite why he should chase through the jungle of political inertia, bureaucratic bungling and ineptitude, for the sake of a few album sales beggars credulity.

Geldof's "get up and do" gospel imperative for the less fortunate came from watching the BBC Nine O'clock News of 23 October 1984, when Michael Buerk had delivered in speech and picture a stunning report on the Ethiopian famine. He had watched this with his girlfriend Paula Yates. They had resolved they must do something.

As Bob said then, and repeated to me in November 1990, "Either you do or you don't."

Paula decided she would raise £2,000 from friends and acquaintances. Bob did not demur but he had larger thoughts, and these centred on the powerful music world. He thought he would gather the major British music stars into one big publicity-ridden recording session for a special record, that would raise thousands of pounds. His particular flair and verbal skills enabled him to circumvent many of the usual intermediaries, and with the basic groundwork done, he then had to wait and see if the stars came. And they did.

He followed the British event with an attempt at persuading the American music people to rouse themselves from their slumbers and out of their electrified home fortresses. At first he met with lukewarm responses; there was not the same amount of immediate passionate commitment, and there was hardly a flicker of interest from the management sector of numerous world-rated US mega-stars. However, Geldof is hardly a quitter, and eventually the USA for Africa movement took off.

Both singles, the British-based "Do they Know it's Christmas?" and the American "We are the World", raised enormous sums of money. Geldof became more and more involved with humanitarian relief work. For a time his already declining music output was very much forgotten. And the Boomtown Rats disbanded, although there was to be a partial re-forming for the Live Aid event that took place on 13th July 1985.

Live Aid provided the "event" of "events" as it seemed almost the whole world community watched the musical deliberations that took place in London and Philadelphia, and that raised collossal global awareness and, more important, monies. But Geldof was to say then, and later,

"I wish I'd never had anything to do with Live Aid."

He was thirty-three when it all took place, possessed of enormous energy, a fast talker, unwilling to suffer fools gladly, and equally unprepared to doff the cap to anyone unless they saw the effort for what it was – an attempt to help people with nothing.

At the time of the event he had an enormous emotional response. "The enormity of it, a million or more things hit me at once, like it was happening, like people in China and elsewhere were with us there and then, 'live', no recording."

But why the hesitation, the regret? "It's down to what people remember." Geldof feared people would think of the style and not the content; and who would question that this has not been the case? Live Aid has become enshrined in rock history as one of its main happenings, with people recalling the musicians, the enormous crowds, and the amazing technological feat of linking the world. But Geldof wanted Live Aid remembered for its original aim, and he hoped that it would continually remind people of the never-ending conflict against hunger and poverty.

Geldof will discuss the time-honoured questions about evil, and undeserved suffering, but in the Live Aid context he says, "I don't know when people talk about God or no God, about God and famine, and starving, and suffering, but I know man is killing hundred of millions of people."

But I fancy he worries that he might join in the endless waffle on what "ought to be done", and much of his success, and charm, comes from assaulting the battalions of the debaters. "All the time you must stop yourself getting cynical, sceptical is fine. You know we need a radical overhaul of the way we behave, our systems are a manifestation of us. Jefferson said all men were created equal, which means all equally created – all nonsense in a real sense, we are not brought into the world equally."

He reveals that his "big" ideas for raising money and world consciousness were in reality only relative to Paula's, for if she had thought in terms of £2,000, then his figure was just over £70,000, and at first he thought it would come from a hit record, and money perhaps given to Save The Children or Oxfam, whatever. It would have been his gesture.

But he realizes he tapped into something – the "mysterious mood of a moment" – that saw a valuable and positive idea grow behond any initial reasonable expectation.

In the end, of course, it isn't a case of wishing he had "never had anything to do with Live Aid", or the myriad of things that followed, for the people with nothing did receive a little, but the whole affair took its toll from Geldof.

Yet he admits he has seen things, experienced much, that few of humankind will ever really know. In the end he has to find his own personal warmth. He told *Q Magazine* in 1990, "But ultimately I will probably remember the Eighties for having my two daughters. That's what I'll remember and enjoy most."

And he said to me, "What's it all about – this gigantic misery? I've done something, I guess, I'll not stop asking 'why' until I die – the terrible things that have and are being done. I rarely understand and at the same time I rarely excuse. You don't have to go there and see, like I did, what's on our TV screens every now and then. People do terrible things to each other."

"Feel so real?" – With people. With actual things. With doing. That is the Geldof way. It has more than a hint of the Gospel which Jesus spoke and brought.

10

HANNE KROGH and
SISSEL KYRKJEBO

Letting music talk

"I had to find time just to think and pray. And then I remember I suddenly felt as if I was being kicked from behind, and my protest was over. I felt freed, and have felt that way ever since."

Hanne Krogh

"I sing because I am happy, and I want to ensure it remains that way. The last thing I want is a loss of control over what I do . . . I don't want a commercial bandwagon taking me along with it."

Sissel Kyrkjebo

The Norwegian musical world is rife with testifying Christians. Among the large artist contingent are Hanne Krogh and Sissel Kyrkjebo.

Those endowed with a good memory and an especial knowledge of Eurovision Song Contest winners should remember that Hanne Krogh, apart from being a major star in Scandinavia, sang Norway to one of her rare dizzy moments in the Contest, winning the 1986 event.

I met Hanne at the excellent Norwegian, Skjaegardsgospel Festival at Kragero, where I had already talked to Andrae Crouch (p. 35). The Festival, which is run by two strong Christians – Tron Sannum Mathisen and his assistant Morten Skjaevestad – is much smaller that Britain's Greenbelt, but some 12,000 came over the weekend in 1990. The site is compact and there is a mixing that was long ago left behind by Greenbelt as it steadily climbed to its current staggering attendance of 25,000-plus. The event reached out into the local town with concerts, open-air happenings and a procession of witness. Except for some specifically Christian gatherings, such as the Sunday morning service, it is a music-based event. Hanne was present, not because she was a billed singer, but simply because the event is an important one on the Norwegian calendar, and she is a Christian. The power of the event in Norway is demonstrated by over a hundred home journalists covering the event for a plethora of newspapers, with many giving the event front-and back-page coverage, and even some middle-page spreads.

Hanne's story of personal faith is of particular interest for those who find the journey into such a commitment riddled with apparent problems. Hanne was initially turned off from enquiring too deeply by what she saw as obstructionist expressions of Christianity. She found people too sure, too overbearing. Those she met did not show a sense of search or questioning.

The "faith" she sensed from those whom she met seemed too difficult, not within her possibilities, and to quote her, "You feel from some people that they've taken out an option on God. You feel they are saying that God is theirs. And I didn't know the language they used. I remember I tried to write a song about it, and in this I said 'Are You for me who doesn't know You?' "

For a while, many blocks seemed to hamper her spiritual journey as she hungered for truths that she suspected lay in the Christian faith. Yet, of course, she had a full work schedule, and time passed and she was no further forward.

However, she continued thinking and enquiring about the faith. "I think I had to find time just to think and pray. And then I remember I suddenly felt as if I was being kicked from behind, and my protest was over. I felt freed, and have felt that way ever since. Even then, I didn't want to be pushed, and it took some time before I could come out and speak about my experience and how I was.''

At the time of our meeting, she felt it was *the* moment when she could really come out and say she was for Jesus, and do so without a backward look. But it had taken time and God had been so patient and gracious.

Sissel is very much the Norwegian mega-star, and someone who pulls no punches on radio and television in clearly establishing her Christian beliefs. While she is forceful in her media and stage presentation, as a person she has a humility that is momentarily disarming, until you've had several long chats. In Norway she has had a string of hit records, with her Christmas album achieving the amazing sale of 500,000-plus, in a population of just over four million.

In her twenties, striking in looks and build, she has always had a belief of sorts, ''Ever since I was very small, though my family were not especially religious. I was sixteen when I took Jesus as my Saviour, and so confessed my faith openly.''

She insists that there is a private personal side to her belief, yet is aware of the importance of openly stating her allegiance. ''In a way it is not natural to me. I can get tongue-tied, but I believe that everything has had a plan in my life. Lots of things have happened to me and I am so thankful.''

Sissel prefers letting her music talk. ''I sing music that I can stand for and believe. So I sometimes sing hymns and I have a special relationship with what they are saying, so I can sing them.''

As she rightly points out, she is not known as a Gospel singer, but when, for instance, she sings with the marvellous Oslo Gospel Choir on a television programme, and performs "Amazing Grace", then there is no doubt about her spiritual allegiance. Some would say that her witness is all the more powerful in this scenario. And when asked, or interviewed, there is no hedging or avoiding an open statement of her personal faith in Christ.

Sissel has a remarkable voice, reminiscent of the early Joan Baez of the 1960s, possessing a vocal purity that grabs and draws tears from this writer. She has a remarkable ease of presence, and circumvents all age barriers, such is the power that emanates from her total giving.

She could surely take Britain or America by storm, yet there is a reticence, though lesser Norwegian artists have gained European and Stateside contracts. "I'm not worried by this kind of possible fame. I sing because I am happy, and I want to ensure it remains that way. The last thing I want is a loss of control over what I do, where I am not responsible, and someone else decides what is important. I don't want a commercial bandwagon taking me along with it."

She feels that she doesn't have to hurry and "if it happens, then it happens", but it will surely happen because she will feel led into a wider geographical field for her rich talent.

Should universal fame come her way, then it must be part of God's plan, and not that of a record corporation's accountancy department.

During the festive season of 1990, Sissel joined other Norwegian "Christian" artists for a special show that was broadcast throughout Norway a few weeks later. It was not only another platform for her amazing ability, and witness, but also showed to all that for many of Norway's famed singers – Jesus lives!

11

GARTH HEWITT

Troubador

"I am uneasy when people thank God and yet do not see where their calling should lead."

In the past Garth Hewitt has stressed that his relationship with Jesus Christ has continued and developed. He has talked of understanding more of the Gospel's nature. There has been emphasis on the essential freedom of the Gospel, that we are offered "fullness of life" and not another set of restrictions.

Garth recalls his early days in the faith, a time when he was a university student, on his way into the ministry of the Church of England. He recalls the impression made on him by Professor H.R. Rookmaaker of the Free University of Amsterdam. "He said, talking about the death of Christ, 'Jesus Christ did not die simply to make us Christians, that's not enough – He died to make us humans!' I find that very profound. Without being in a relationship with the God who has created us, we are not being *fully* human. We were created in his image. We were *meant* to have a relationship with him. Unless we have that relationship we are losing out, we are limited by our own selfishness and our own ego. We've got the blinkers on, and we're narrow-minded because we can't see beyond our own horizons!"

The upshot of all this was stressed in the songs he wrote and performed. A lover of rock'n'roll, and in tune with contemporary trends, Hewitt brought a delicious touch of pop culture reality into a religious scene so often visited by pleasant singer-songwriters who were trying to reach people with their three-chord suprises.

In any case, he always looked a rock'n'roller rather than a pleasant religious soul. And after studies at Durham and the London College of Divinity (now St John's, Nottingham), he served as a curate at St Luke's, Maidstone, before joining the Church Pastoral-Aid Society as a full-time evangelist with the specific role of singer and songwriter. He was as at home in the church schoolroom as in a club on Tyneside or in trouble-torn Belfast. One week he would be at the Royal Albert Hall, and another in Dartmoor prison.

If you look back, at what he has said in past times, you will find Garth saying, "I think that what I'm trying to do is simply *reflect* in my music the things *I believe*. I want to also entertain, because what is the point of music if it isn't entertaining? *But* I want my music to be *more* than entertainment. There's a certain style of folk music that is very lyric-orientated while other music emphasizes the sound and the lyrics hardly play a part. With *my* approach the lyrics are a crucial part. What makes it specifically Christian is that *I* am a Christian. There are two different types of Christian musicians; those who see themselves primarily as entertainers (who happen to be Christians) and those who are trying to communicate their faith (and so it happens that their art form is music)."

He felt that it was much harder for someone to present a Christian art form in rock music, but stressed his own preference for those musicians with a strong vocal sound and who, at the same time, were lyric-orientated. He stressed how he wanted through his music to raise certain questions in people's minds about life and truth. "I feel that music doesn't have the same effect as preaching, and therefore, one doesn't necessarily have the *same* response. Music is very much for *sowing* seeds of ideas . . . I get people coming back to me years after I've sung a piece to tell me that it meant a lot to them, and if I'd stood up and preached on the same subject I'm sure it wouldn't have stuck in their minds so long!"

Garth was conscious that he was a trifle unusual. Here he was, a clergyman, and at the same time a singer. "Hopefully I can bring to bear on my lyrics *more* of a theological *insight* than someone who hasn't my background . . . Often an evangelist's lifestyle can look very unreal. That's why during my chatter in between my songs I try to be honest and really human."

Many of these quotes come from an interview Garth had with a friend of mine, Paul Davis, and as I read them back to him, on a cold Sunday afternoon, he did a quick think-back, and then answered the central pivot of my questioning – how does he see himself now? He is still a singer-songwriter, still an Anglican priest, but older, perhaps wiser, having seen and experienced so many things over the past twenty years.

"Yes, I feel I have been on a journey. Unless you stay in a time warp, and some people do, you must advance, and develop. God offers so many possibilities; and yes, the Eighties decade was very fruitful, and I've been challenged in my faith by the poverty I've seen, the injustice I'm aware of, and have had to realize that if faith is credible, if there is good faith, then it has to take into account the fact over two-thirds of the world's population know not wealth, but poverty."

Garth Hewitt the singer-songwriter remains. There is no diminution of his enthusiasm for concerts, or making records. "I am a singer who sings about Jesus, and anyone who comes to my concerts is soon made aware of this, if it is not known beforehand. I could I suppose be some kind of lecturer, show videos, films, and so on, but, no, I am a musician. I like writing and singing stories. I sing about the wider understanding of the Gospel that is now mine. I can sing about religion, but I mean I am singing about all of life.''

He rather fancies the title ''troubadour'', and thinks of some periods in Christian history where certain musicians entertained and at the same time drew people's attention to what was happening in the world.

Garth develops his current role and musical identity under what he terms ''the story-telling tradition'': here, he will draw attention to basic gospel truths as they are seen within the life-and-death situations he has witnessed around the world. In the last decade he made three important journeys. He went to India; he was in Uganda during civil strife; he visited the black townships in South Africa. It has made his faith more rounded, more true, he believes, to the total dimension of the Gospel.

And his songs have continually reflected what he has seen, and how he has reacted theologically. All this might not have been his lot if certain moves to push his work on the general music world stage had not failed around the early years of the last decade. It was then that Garth, along with Nutshell, and to some degree Adrian Snell, were among a small group of Christian musicians who many fancied could emerge out of what some called ''the religious ghetto'' and really make the Gospel count in the area of general music. But although Cliff Richard produced an album for him, and several catchy singles, it didn't happen. And for a while he went through difficult times that forced him to reconsider the nature of his calling.

That ''Calling'' was to receive its flesh and blood with Garth's increasing social and political involvement. He came to see that true faith in the Gospel is not an individualistic happiness spree, oblivious of other people. Nor would he see the word "comfortable" as applying to the faith. He would see conversion bringing people into a greater awareness of work that needs to be done. For him, there is no faith without community involvement. He groans at endless adulation for God and Jesus from musicians who themselves lack any kind of practical involvement for their neighbours. He came to see everything revolving around a Christ who has gone before, and is found, and is not someone who is dragged into situations we have created.

Being a singer-songwriter has meant adopting a tougher stance, and this "troubadour" is very much cast in a prophetic role. He doesn't pretend it is easy. Yet he believes it is his calling that he should present through his lyrics, life as he has seen it, faith as he sees it as relevant to those situations. "I would like to see more people picking this up. On the whole people are good at giving their testimony, and pointing people to Jesus, but it rarely has a social and political extension. I think it is a tougher role than just going up on stage and singing a very individual testimony."

In his view, personalized faith is the dominant heresy of our time. "And I am uneasy when people thank God and yet do not see where their calling should lead."

By halfway through 1991 *his* calling received another album dressing. *Lonesome Troubadour* took the listener through numerous situations, from Brazil, to the Lebanese and Jewish communities, to China. It reflected the varied liturgical worlds that Garth had encountered on his many travels.

His love for music remains undiminished. "Yes, it is still important. I'm still writing songs. I welcome anyone to come and hear me. I like crossing boundaries. I think there is a place for someone like me, and there should be others. I think with the right songs, the right story, you can reach anyone, Christians or not. I don't hide things."

It seems a trifle "wet" to say that the scene is better for a Garth Hewitt; but it is.

12

LEVINE HUDSON

Total involvement

"It isn't always easy, sometimes I feel I'm not in a position even to kneel. I have pleaded to God that he might give me strength."

"Feel so real" to Levine Hudson means one thing – singing gospel. It's something she has always done, and she intends it should stay that way. Such is the power of her voice that many have seen her as a young Aretha Franklin, the great American soul singer, from a church background, and with several incredible gospel albums in her extensive song catalogue.

For her, the record route has been not through a religious company but rather via a major British group, Virgin. Right from the start her immediate appeal has been on the general music stage, with her records heard across the broad spectrum of radio programming.

She's known for her determination to see that her career is not corrupted by the dubious machinations of the pop business, and equally she is very much to the point when she says, "I have spoken to singers in America, and not naming names, it doesn't matter to them, they're in it for the cash."

When I met her one afternoon at Virgin Records in Harrow Road, London, she seemed slight of build, initially hesitant, blessed with a radiant smile, and not at first glance someone who might insist on God's guidance to direct her recording and performing career. But then, first surmises can be very wrong. And this was one case.

Levine seemed to be under the impression that any writer or journalist might doubt her motives, and, at very least might wonder why Virgin should sign a gospel singer, rather than say a floor and rap artist for yet another one-directional twelve-inch smasheroo.

So I came right out with the fact that I was a Christian, that among other things I wrote books, and wished through some of my writing to encourage young Christians in the faith, while, at the same time, to make people in music land aware that they are not alone if they are Christians.

That eased matters. Levine seemed a little nonplussed that a pop writer might share the many things of faith with her. Curled up in a chair in a slightly defensive body position, she unwrapped herself, and smiled broadly, once the news had sunk in. That said, I was aware that although we could talk about gospel music, and we did, we still came at faith from a different cultural setting, and indeed a different experience of the Christian community.

She admitted she could be stubborn, but it was all part of the overall demand she felt the Gospel laid upon her. She had no wish that she should be translated into the record production machine, that her essential "Gospel" should be effectively satanized.

To anyone who has ever signed a record contract, and then gone into the studios, that comment of hers has force. Marketing demands often lead to a tinkering with material. For Levine, the base of all things is simply "that I remain faithful to Jesus".

Her sense of feeling real comes from the total involvement in what she does. Her desire is to oversee all things, to underwrite everything with prayer, the one ingredient that makes all things possible.

Yes indeed, the technical side is present for any artist, and that is neutral, so there is either a good mix or there is not, and an engineer is either good or not, and a producer either is or not; but whatever the professionalism, empathy can still play a part. Levine could not ensure that her recording personnel were signed-up Christians but she could insist that her standards were both professional and fitting for the high claims of the Gospel.

Also, for Levine, as indeed for any artist, there is always the problem of recreating a "live" feel in the cold formless state of a studio, often hidden well below ground, or part of an endless corridor belt, with silence ensuing everywhere, in itself an atmosphere that has to be counteracted once work has begun.

"I think I'm essentially a 'live' performer, that I can sing properly, if you like, without boosting. I suppose I do have retakes! But not many. I go ahead, adapt, and lay the tracks down. I know how I feel about God and Jesus, and I think that before I sing and record."

And she adds, "I sing from the heart. I'm not into the crazy scene where you go on and expect mixes and mixes. If I do things again, it's not because I am finicky, more because I know how something should be, how I see it, anyway."

When she speaks directly of her faith, she becomes very animated. It is a source of great joy that she has a relationship with God. To me it is not a take-it-or-leave-it faith. It changes you. I think some people are scared of it, because it does demand, even if the gift of life is free.

"I must tell of my faith. Yes, I have grown up with my believing parents, and yes, I have a church, it is where my father is minister, and it is the Church of God, in Vauxhall, London. But it is my own response to Christ. To me, it is important that I am at church. When I recorded my first album there was a mix arranged for a Sunday but I said no. In life, I need a base and I have it. It isn't always easy, sometimes I feel I'm not in a position to kneel even. I have pleaded to God that he might give me strength.''

13

JOHN LEES

Seeds that produce flowers

Barclay James Harvest

"I'm into straightforward worship, no frills or fancies. I mean our church is busy, there are lots of young people, there is music and drama, and we find God. I do enjoy it. I really do."

During the tour of Barclay James Harvest through Britain and Europe, which lasted for some three or four months, vocalist and guitarist John Lees took his Bible with him with the aim of reading it through from cover to cover. "It's a heck of a read," is his comment, but 1990 was not long enough, for he went into the succeeding year at only the beginning of the New Testament. It was not that he had slacked or gone from day to day without reading, as the group's magnificent bus had wended its way from city to city. It had just absorbed him. For John, this "read" was part of his newly found enthusiasm for what has always been with him – his Christian belief.

Quite calmly he says that really his religious story is nothing exceptional. He has no dramatic story to tell. He takes me back to his childhood when he and his sister attended the local parish church in Oldham. He belonged to the cub scouts and went on church sorties to the seaside and the countryside. He remembers there was distinct religious allegiance within the family, and one that crossed the denominational boundaries.

The other day he drove past the church where he had

attended but which now is, sadly, up for sale. It also reminded him that in his early teens he had come to a point when confirmation had been suggested. His parents had not pushed John or his sister to make a decision either way. As it happened, he was not confirmed, and the upshot was that he left the church; it seems there was no choice. So he was claimed for elsewhere by other members of the family, in this instance a mix of Methodism and Congregationalism. When he was sixteen, he became embroiled in music, and the church got rather left behind. John had new things to interest him and they seemed exciting.

He was perturbed at the course his sister took. She became interested in the Mormons, but after a year or so she had the self-will and strength to leave. John made music. He kept away from drink and drugs; they didn't seem necessary, even if some people might have thought so. By the time he was nineteen and at art school, he had met Woolly "Stewart" Wolstenholme, and was playing in The Blues Keepers. That led the way to recruiting two members of another local group, Les Holroyd and Mel Pritchard, and from all this Barclay James Harvest was born. Since those days a great number of albums have been issued, with many charting high in the British album listings, while in France and Germany the group (minus Woolly who had left along the way) have mega-star rating with the top of the tops.

Along the way, and through the years, BJH, as they are commonly known, or The Barclays, have intrigued some with many a song lyric that has a religious twist, or reflects an area of social concern. In the former, "Hymn" and "He said Love" are two of the most blatant examples of John pushing his beliefs strongly, "Hymn" has become an anthem while of the latter he says, "The others didn't play on it, it wasn't necessary." He doesn't think the other two rate it that highly, but in a group "give and take" must exist. He puts it this way; "You get to a stage, and you just do."

A few years back, partly as a result of his children attending the local church, he found his way back into regular Sunday worship. At first, apart from the vicar no one really knew of his rock fame, so as he says, "No one wanted me to write a rock'n'roll Christmas musical!" He was content with being there, savouring the basic Christian worship of the Church of England rite, from family service to morning prayer to the Communion service. "For me, it's enough to think of God, Jesus. To relax in His presence. Perhaps I am a little selfish in not participating in more general church activities."

He has met good people, kind people. He has found peace of mind. He says that prayer has been the focal point of his Christian living. "I've always prayed actually, even during times when I was not a church-goer. I'm really into it. A useful device!"

I fancy he feels a little self-conscious, although I may have made him that way during our talk, that there is no big story for the telling. He puts it this way; "I'm into straightforward worship, no frills or fancies. I mean our church is busy, there are lots of young people, there is music and drama, and we find God." And, yes, he adds disarmingly, "I do enjoy it. I really do."

Yet it would be a little much if everyone had a "pop" story to tell, for most people find their worship, as it ought to be, a meeting with their Maker and celebrating His love in Jesus and knowing the power of the Spirit.

I've travelled France with BJH, and seen the reaction they get. Probably most of the 10,000-plus that hear the band in such a part of the world, in one of those enormous

French gymnasiums, are not too conscious that John is a Christian as they wave their hands to "Hymn", or applaud and sing with "Life is for Living". But that is the way it is. He's not against sharing his faith, but has never gone out of his way either to adorn the glossy religious magazines or to have his name blazened abroad in a tabloid check-down on the faith people.

John Lees is a quiet, thoughtful, reflective person, and also highly intelligent and well-read. In the end it would be better that the kingdom has seeds that produce flowers, rather than a host of instant Jesus-proclaiming music people who soon wither and perish as they turn to the next fad.

I left him with the thought that at long last his Bible reading would take him into the exciting world of the New Testament. His is a voice that doesn't trumpet his beliefs, but there is no mistaking his inner joy.

14

GEOFF MANN

Outside edge

"I'm amused now that I thought God didn't come into anything – that was when I was in Form 4B."

The Arts Centre Group with its British headquarters in Short Street, London, provided the venue for my meeting with Geoff Mann, singer, songwriter, and latterly a Church of England curate living in Salford, Lancashire.

The ACG, as it it known, is an association of Christians professionlly involved in the world of the arts, media and entertainment. Its aim is to help its members to work effectively as Christians in their chosen disciplines and so to make a distinctive contribution to our culture. On Thursday evenings it runs a "meeting house" with a cabaret and food, and it was to this that Geoff came and performed.

In past times Geoff did not gain major pop success, but all the same he belonged to a much-advertised group called Twelfth Night, with their music credited in appropriate musical encyclopedias, and which drew sizeable crowds. When he left the band he formed his own group, and this has gone through several reincarnations, while from time to time Geoff has played solo dates. Five albums have come through one of these Mann musical expressions, and although he sometimes plays the church mission, he continues his strong association with the rock club venue, in which he is accepted as a highly talented performer and a very good writer of lyrics and tunes.

He likes to use the term "outside edge" to describe his work. He sees himself playing and spreading the good news amongst those who are often ignored by conventional bodies. For, he believes, and he gives practical flesh to his conviction, that people in rock clubs and disco halls have as much right as anyone to sense and know the possibilities that are offered in Jesus.

Underlying Geoff's attitude is a wonder that he has been so used by God, and stronger still, that he has been called to be God's vehicle.

Unlike many rock musicians, Geoff has strong professional qualifications in another area: he has a degree in art. However, it was while he was at art school that he took his teenage love of music into something more tangible as he and others made music, and he eventually joined Twelfth Night.

At the time he was a Christian. He had in any case had a Christian home background, but there had been a period when he had run away from the faith, although he always kept before him the truth that Jesus had died for him.

He calls himself a "questioning animal" and while he was with Twelfth Night he was eagerly trying to learn more about what Christianity says.

This declaration was expressed in a more intense form when he decided to leave the group. Geoff speaks with much passion about music: "I love music, I love rocking, I love gigs. I like to write and play music. I want to write about things, not love songs, unless it is about God's love. And if someone finds faith through what I do, then it's great."

One reason for his departure lay with his overall indecision, even uncertainty, over the nature of God's call. "I said to myself that I had to sort things out. I had to go home and work out the future." Fortunately he has an understanding life's partner, and also his local vicar was an enormous help. "I think he was someone to whom I could put my questions and not feel that I might be laughed at."

He became what he terms a "house husband", and with Jane working he kept home and looked after the first child in their marriage, Thomas. It was a time to let go with God, and ask to know his will.

Much of his intensified searching was directly related to Jane's somewhat laid-back method of increasing his awareness of God. Daily she gave him a Bible quote, often spoken over the telephone, as he would phone from a gig. And she had become a regular church-goer.

The immediate search was over when he realized that God was calling him into the ordained ministry of the Church of England. Even that, though, was not without problems, for at first he failed to satisfy the selection committee; but his bishop overturned these decisions, and Geoff has been immensely grateful for this confidence in him.

He became more or less "an Open University type student", for he worked from home, and faced "long essays, and 7,000-word plus projects, and then there was a placement."

All the time that this was happening he kept plugging away with music. In 1989 he was ordained, and he celebrated by launching a new band. He says, "I have to write what's right", which is one of Geoff's often cryptic comments. "I like to sing about faith. I want people to know Christ died for them. I want God to use my musical offering. I want people to hear the good news. I think what God offers encompasses all things, politics, love, whatever, you name it. My writing is a serious thing, to me it's an extension of things, It's finding new shapes and basic formulas. It takes time."

Geoff talks about God in an uncomplicated fashion. He talks about faith as though it is the most natural thing in the world. He doesn't bore or grate.

He doesn't see God calling him to be something that he is not, and nor does he see the man of faith as a person who tries to be this and that, as a means of winning people into the Kingdom. "You have to trust him. I'm amused now that I thought God didn't come into anything – that was when I was in form 4B!"

Now Geoff is the father of three. He is also learning the perils and joys of parish work, but rejoicing that his music ministry has continued unhindered. He has no idea where God will lead him but he is convinced that God has much use for him. "I always marvel at that. If I was God, I wouldn't bother with me!"

15

MARIA McKEE

In touch with reality

"It's like God had given me this gift, and for me to take all the praise for it would be ridiculous."

Her home background provided a varied religious fare, from transcendental meditation to Catholicism to the Baptists to the Charismatics. In the musical realm her half-brother Bryan was in the mainstream of American music in the late 1970s, and he played with the legendary West Coast outfit, Love, of Arthur Lee connection. Maria read avidly stories of people with powerful lifestyles. She loved the works of Tennessee Williams and delved into books on the history of vaudeville.

Music was ever present, and partly through her brother's connections, she met numerous famous names of the time. By the time she was sixteen she was amazing people with her convincing blues singing. On Independence Day 1982, Lone Justice was born. It was the result of endless hours she had spent practising her vocals, and writing songs. She had sung with her brother's own band, and had attracted a following that had spread to musicians and those in the music business whose job it is to find new acts.

Lone Justice albums rang to her exultant, powerful vocals. Her Gospel background was ever present. A song such as "You are the Light" was raw power, while "I found Love" could not fail to thrill even the hardened. It gave her, and the group, a brief taste of being in the British charts. The song itself could be taken in several forms but as a Gospel expression it was vivid testimony without the forced nature of some Jesus music. It was genuine. It was whole.

It almost becomes a secondary, even a forgotten fact, but for true artists the real love of their career is song. Not unexpectedly in a cynical age, artists who stress their passion for music and place making money second, receive from writers a long-drawn-out snort of derision.

In areas more concerned with "message-giving", music comes a poor second. This is true of much Christian music that has emanated from many sources since the early Sixties. In this area there have been countless artists who pay less attention to the genre in which they work than to the effect they intend causing. Such performers will sing in any style, adopt any musical or recorded sound, so long as it means that they can reach people with the thoughts they wish to convey. Unfortunately most fail in their task. Music is not to be corrupted, though within the wider confines of the music industry it may often be seen as no more than a product – a stock item with no more intrinsic mystery than a packet of soap powder.

Maria McKee knows both worlds well. She has loved music with intensity almost, it would seem, from the time she could identify musical sound. She is someone who was raised with a Christian background, and has at times prefaced her musical love with God-talk, but she has little sympathy with those who masquerade as music lovers in order to preach a message. It seems that this is one reason why in more recent times, she has curtailed her statements of faith, lest she be unjustly categorized or alternatively find herself pursued by those forever questioning why she does this or that.

At the same time she sang a song called "Soup, Soap and Salvation", a protest against some religious practices of which she despaired. It centred on supposed help and aid for those who were in need. She observed the awfulness of the form of "giving" by bargaining with those who had little or nothing that they could barter with save their own threatened identity; a bargain by which they were only fed after they had been subjected to a hell-fire preach. Even more, should the hungry close their eyes during message time, and drift away into the land of dreams, they would be given their marching orders. Rightly, she observed, this was no true love without cost, this was greed.

Her work was seen in a God-context. She spoke of her singing in these terms: "I know that I have a gift. I'm not going to deny the fact that I can sing and that God has gifted me, but I don't really think of it as being me. It's like if somebody gives you a present, and you say, 'Hey, I'm great, I've got this great present!' It's just a present you have. It's like God has given me this gift, and for me to take all the praise for it would be ridiculous."

By the summer of 1989 she was very much a solo artist, with her own self-titled album. In her interviews, she talked of the pressures she had undergone in constant touring, and of how life had become somewhat sour. She had also striven to ensure that she remained in touch with reality, and so would not join the fraternity of stars who lose touch with the basics, cocooned by success and the protective entourage that clings to them. Maria was driven to say: "It's important to be a human being. It's important to be able to look someone else in the eye, and to have a personal balance. I'm not into the alien types running around. Beam me up to reality, Scottie!"

During 1990 her life took an unexpected lift. She topped the British charts with "Show me Heaven". It could have been a gospel song. Almost before the first minute had passed, we were hearing about saving grace. Actually, the song was from the soundtrack of the Tom Cruise film *Days Of Thunder*. Initially, she says, she didn't like it. The original lyrics were bad. When she communicated the message, and was refused changes, she turned down the project. Later, there was a turnaround and her wishes were granted. Her first move meant the song title was altered from "Secret Fire" to "Show me Heaven". What she described as an original "overblown lush ballad", became a song that can be taken in various ways.

Her faith remains, albeit hidden from public gaze, and not so much for viewing as it was when she came with Lone Justice a few years back. She spends time with Bono (Lone Justice supported U2 on their 1985 US tour), is great friends with Maire Ni Bhraonain of Clannad, and is on the verge of big career happenings, especially since 1991, when she entered into new record contractual arrangements.

16

MIKE PETERS

A million times more happiness

The Alarm

"I think I've learnt how the quiet and more subtle approach is the one that really helps people. And I present Christianity as a way to follow."

"I know I'll find you, I know I'll find you."

I cannot say I was surprised to find, in the early 1980s, that Mike Peters, lead singer and chief songwriter of a rather unruly, loud, post-punk outfit called the Alarm, had a fair degree of interest in Christian matters.

There were all kinds of clues. The band would gig often as support to the fast-emerging Irish band U2, whose Christian affiliations had been announced by the music weekly *Sounds* (rather than applauding, *Sounds* had decided to label the band "mad"). And since it appeared that both bands intermingled to a fair degree, it could be assumed that Bono and Mike would talk religion. Certainly in the "live" context Mike would join Bono and they would spiritedly sing Dylan's somewhat overdone song "Knocking on Heaven's Door".

There were early songs with a religious twist, for instance, "The Stand", the group's third single. Mike claimed that the band was endeavouring to champion the cause of the individual. He urged people to withstand the knocks and bad things, and insist on their uniqueness.

Again, the early songs had a stridency about them, and

it was no surprise to note that the debut album was called "Declaration". There was a pseudo-religious nature about the work. There was a spiritual ring about it. This was not so clear when it came to the album "Strength", where everything seemed rather man-centred, as though man could save himself.

But there would be a change – the "Christian" thing would infiltrate, as Mike would learn to trust more and more in his convictions, and find the strength to plough his own furrow. As he fought for his beliefs, so too it seems that he drew the attention of those who would have liked him and the band to be no more than some kind of religious vehicle, without their own way of doing things. At the same time, he was conscious of thrusting things at the audience, demanding that they might believe because he did, rather than that they should make their own journey.

Once, in early times, Mike said, "There's an awful lot of people who would do anything I say. If I said, 'Let's all jump in the fire tomorrow!', some of them would."

He began clearly to define his role: "I'm to say, what do you think about it?"

In November 1990, Mike sits in the office of IRS Records, in the outer area of London's Soho.

The ostensible purpose of our meeting on this occasion is that Mike should take me through the group's first compilation album. This is comprised of tracks taken from the group's four albums of the Eighties, plus a few other recordings. The meeting is one of many interviews he will give so that the public is fully aware of this new Alarm release.

He is in a good mood, a little rushed, for he hopes to catch a train from Euston to see his beloved Manchester

United in action for a midweek cup game – the interview cannot ramble on too long!

The spikey-haired rock singer answers the odd question or two, but the main bulk of the conversation centres on Greenbelt 1990, at which he appeared, and on the group, and on our common love for Jesus.

Mike's Christian experience goes back to the outset of the Eighties. It was then that he put pen to paper and chords to music, as he resolved to present music fans with the big hoax of Christian faith; but as it turned out, he was claimed before his song "Shout to the Devil" could make the recording studio.

He had intended telling people that the Christian faith had nothing to offer. "It was a real put-down of the Bible and Jesus. But I was asking the questions."

However, he also decided that it would be flippant merely to launch an attack on the Christian faith without actually finding out more about it. At this time his understanding and awareness simply came from memories of Sunday school days, and lessons at school. So he consulted friends and acquaintances, and to his surprise he found that some of them were Christians. Many of his questions were answered, and in such a way that he began to take notice of what the Gospel was about.

He talks of receiving a book in the post. "I was going to Liverpool for the weekend and just remember some voice in my head saying, 'You musn't leave that book behind, you've got to pick it up and take it with you' ".

He took the book with him, and read it on the train. He remembers little of what it said, but if definitely challenged him. He felt a response welling up inside of him, and he knew he could not wage war against this Jesus. There were tears of contrition, of joy, and of peace. It was a moment and a time that would never leave him.

In a way he found the whole thing strange. In career terms he was faring well. People said that prospects for him and the group were considerable, and really it seemed to outward and worldly appearances, that he had no need of religion. Yet, once "aware", he felt it was akin to receiving a million times more happiness.

He told the band of his belief. They were not bowled over by the news, but they respected what he said. In fact, he felt he should tell everyone. And, in common with Cliff in his early days as a Christian, he wondered if he should give up his music career, but he felt he should be where he was, influential, and possessing an ability to speak of his faith to millions worldwide.

In our conversation that winter afternoon, Mike was relaxed, still joyous in his faith, aware of life's preciousness, and recounting some sadnesses that had come into his life in recent times, including the deaths of his sister (from a brain haemorrhage) and his father.

"I find my faith getting stronger and stronger. I think I've been through quite a few life experiences since that day when I felt Christ was for me. I have no hesitation in saying I am a Christian. It's now part of my life-blood, this faith of mine.

"People come and say this and that to me, and I know some people might be saying why am I doing this and that. But we all have to face those who don't really understand what we are doing."

He muses once more on those first heady days of faith. "If I was going to put it down, see what I found out! Oh, I said 'Who is this Jesus?' And I said no one has answers. I don't think I thought there could be answers from mere people. But then I came to him – Jesus."

But he hesitates in coming over too strong, and expresses how he has found some Christians overpowering.

"They've even frightened me. I think I've learnt how the quiet and more subtle approach is the one that really helps people. And I present Christianity as a way to follow."

He talks a great deal about balance, of being himself, of finding space to grow, and of letting his music quietly express the faith without throttling people to the extent that they turn off both The Alarm and the faith.

All that he says comes with an infectious enthusiasm, for his faith is no longer unsure, and he is not worried about people knowing where he stands. Now he says what he believes. And he does so with a quiet, convincing ease that can in no way be construed as mad.

He sings, "I'll know I'll find you" – he has.

17

CLIFF RICHARD

Confident in his faith

"God has given him the gift of communication. I am always impressed by the maturity of the faith he holds."
Bill Latham on Cliff

June 16th 1991 saw the twenty-fifth anniversary of the day when Britain's leading pop star appeared on stage at a Billy Graham campaign, and told the world what had hitherto been mostly known only to his inner circle of friends — that he was a card-carrying Christian.

Many who were there on that evening remember a pop star who became nervous, who sweated a great deal, who none the less was fluent and persuasive. He was young in the faith, and unlike many who can find time to forge ahead, this person had no such luxury. Once he had spoken, the media world descended, and for many months afterwards he told and retold of his conversion, of his hopes and dreams, and how this new assault upon his whole being might affect his career. That story he recounted everywhere, from religious "quality" paper to teenage girl magazine. It seemed that everyone wanted to know. And it appeared that pop stars did not say they were religious.

Numerous books have recorded how he debated whether he should stay with popular music and entertainment, or chase after a teaching career. Of course he stayed with music, and so for a quarter of a century he has been *the* name when it comes to direct Christian witness from within the pop fraternity.

His many books, speeches, radio and television appearances have set the faith before millions, and countless people have become interested, and eventually persuaded, largely through his witness. He has his detractors, and some do not walk the same political path as he does, but surely only a few would refute the simple proposition – that Cliff Richard has stayed with his faith through thick and thin.

Bill Latham has managed Cliff's Christian and personal affairs for a long time. This one-time schoolmaster was largely instrumental in pushing the youngish pop singer toward mainstream orthodox Christian belief; for otherwise Cliff might have gone the way of his mother, Hank Marvin and Liquorice Locking, into the Jehovah's Witness movement.

So Bill has observed from close hand the spiritual and religious path of Cliff. At our meeting to "discuss Cliff", he told me that the great thing about Cliff the Christian, the religious man, was that he was confident in his faith. He hastened to add that this confidence had nothing to do with a sense of "knowing it all", of resting in firm and entrenched positions, which nothing could affect.

Rather, Bill suggested that Cliff had an inner sense of relaxation, that he rested firmly and squarely on the intrinsic Christian statement that God loves.

It was on this that Cliff grounded his sureness. It was something that he personally knew and experienced.

For Bill, Cliff's Christian story has been amazing. Cliff is no intellectual, and is not given to reading weighty theological tomes, yet he is someone who easily grasps and sets out to comprehend what seems puzzling. In a sense this attitude characterizes his music. Cliff only does things well, and whatever the event, small or large, he expects to work things out, and to ensure that everything is done

as it should be. So in matters of faith, too, he knows there
is not a great deal of room for the slipshod and the
half-hearted.

"God has given him the gift of communication," says
Bill. "I am always impressed by the maturity of the faith
he holds." And in this communication, and with his
sureness, Cliff still has room for admitting to some things
he doesn't know, and some questions to which he doesn't
know the answers. And he suggests that Cliff, especially
in early times, has never looked out of place or seemed
ignorant when in the company of greater minds, partly
because of his refreshing honesty, and also because in the
end he has this confidence in the faith.

He recalls the early man of faith. "I think what Cliff
recognized when he met mainstream Christianity,
Crusaders and other groups, was that this was a dimension
of the faith that he hadn't seen before, and it appealed.
The Jehovah's Witnesses were more theoretical and
legalistic. He found a new freedom, it seemed so new. In
the end it was nothing anyone particularly said – it was
an attitude, priority values, relationships."

As Bill pointed out, not too many people have been aware
of the considerable heartache that Cliff went through when
he chose "mainstream" faith as opposed to the Jehovah's
Witness movement. "It did cause disappointment", not
merely to Cliff's much loved mum, but also to his sister
Jackie, who was ardent in the movement.

There were discussions and arguments, and eventually
each went their own way, with decisions and responses
mutually respected. Integrity was found on both sides.
Here was a closely-knit family now divided, yet still
listening and talking.

So the years have passed, and Cliff has often had to
withstand carping even from amongst the religious

community, particularly from those who see modern music as of the devil; but rarely has he chastened, or retaliated against, those who often come with words and shouts totally unworthy of the name of Christ.

Even time has failed to erase certain doubts about the authenticity of his faith. People still say he uses religion to boost general record sales and fill concert halls. Confidence in his faith has given Cliff the courage to withstand the nasties.

But has Cliff manipulated fans? "If he has, then he ought to be criticized, but I don't see any evidence for this," says Bill. "He has always discouraged those who go over the top, and he has pointed people to Christ, not himself."

Obviously much acclaim has come Cliff's way, and it could easily have led him into a false adulation of himself. "I don't think Cliff has ever tried to build a strange mystique but some people have been guilty of creating one. I mean there are churches and vicars who, if you like, just want autographs and he has no time for that at all." That said, there are certainly some religious people, and others, who behave in the most strange fashion in his presence by ceasing to treat him as a person, as a brother in Christ, and rather help to promulgate the "star" image.

In terms of the pop world, as opposed to the Christian scene, Bill sees Cliff meeting a direct need. "Cliff thinks the music-biz needs the uncompromising Christian voice. And in a sense he is disappointed that some other music people who are Christians do not make their voices heard, and so are more up-front. Of course, it might be said that there is another side, for Cliff is well established, and so they might say it's all right for him. Some think they might lose their career if they make direct Christian statements."

Yet of course Cliff risked much when in 1966 he joined

the platform of an American evangelist, and at the very least in the ensuing events he added an extra burden to an already demanding diary. So too he added the unwanted burden of the suspicious people, the questioning media and the general public, who would not settle for the simple story that really, it was just the case that he had accepted Christ.

Yet he soldiers on, much more in joy than sorrow. He has this enormous enthusiasm that is apparent in so many areas, hardly contrived, and giving off 110 per cent, even in the situations that are never his real favourites, such as press calls, and where the same kind of questions invariably are put – "Are you gay?" "Will you marry one day?"

Cliff has a professional commitment, hunger for what some now call, fondly, old-fashioned standards, the simple maxim, "If you are going to do something, then whatever it is, you do it well." Bill talks of Cliff's total dedication to even the smallest of events, and he will go through the same professional soundcheck whether the event is before an audience of 100,000 or a few hundred in a church hall in the back of seeming nowhere.

He has this positive drive, and an ambition to make things better and better. No one would deny that this was part of Cliff's overall show-biz attitude before he knew Jesus and the Christian way, but many would say that his Christian conviction has given all this a steadier base, for his experience of Christ has given him an inner confidence and peace that does not come through record sales and the adulation of fans.

"He is conscious of seeking to know what God wants him to do, and if that involves some chores, then it does. I mean it is a positive advantage when someone like him says, 'I'll enjoy it, even if . . .' "

However, all this seemingly unending appreciation of Cliff should not blind anyone to the fact that Cliff does have his faults, and at a basic level, Bill says he is someone who "talks more than he listens. He is a good chatterer and not a good listener."

But what does the man himself think? His deprecating sense of humour quickly comes into play. He talks of being the oldest teenager in the business, of getting older, of having a genuine "wonder" as to the whys and wherefores of his lasting so long in a music world that creates names and discards them in the space of twelve months. He quickly confirms some of Bill's observations without being asked. "I've never really needed an incentive. I have had to work at things, yes, and pay special attention to my weight and how I look, but I've never had a career nose-dive that some have had, with consequent drastic measures to regain the lost ground."

He talks to me about making himself aware of what else is happening in his life, of deliberately sitting down from time to time and thinking what he might do. There has been an intent to explore every facet of his being so that he can feel he has used and explored what God has given him. He speaks of the difficulty in relentlessly pursuing objectives when often confronted by what the media makes of him.

Underlying all is his belief that his faith has matured and developed. He knows that even twenty-five years of Christian discipleship seems a mere beginning when it comes to spiritual awareness and appreciation. In career terms the old division of gospel and secular has disappeared. There are still the odd gospel tours, and mostly for charity – usually Tear Fund is the beneficiary. But his major concerts now include songs of faith, and often he talks animatedly of how his belief in Jesus has been the precious life-enhancer. This development is seen as part of his maturity and self-confidence. He does not heed any more the "voices" that suggest it might not be a good thing that he should express how he sees things from a Christian perspective.

He takes extra-special delight in knowing that there are so many people in the numerous branches of the entertainment world who have become Christians, or at the very least, are expressing interest in and recognition of Christian things. And outside the glitter and glam of the concert world, he has been very active in bringing together people from all walks of the "biz" to eat, discuss and pray. So far as I know, he is the only person who readily gives time to this kind of friendship and ministry.

Confident in his faith, Cliff knows that we need each other, that Christians need to share their experiences of how God is at work. And in hard times, it is not possible to say that God does not understand, because He always does, for He has been through it, for that is one way of understanding the Cross.

Who knows where the future leads for Cliff? But at least the past has been reasonably clear – it seems to say without doubt that here is someone who has been well used by God to witness in an area that affects so many lives, often with unpleasant consequences. Yet the music world, its industry and workings, its wider ramifications into how purchasers and consumers view its deliberations, is merely a microcosm of life as a whole, as indeed the pages of any daily newspaper will show. Into this world, as into any other part of the wider whole, the light of the Gospel must shine.

Cliff's confidence in the Gospel has been a boon and a blessing for thousands.

18

SAL SOLO

"Just be it!"

"To me my faith is all of my life. It means everything to me. I believe what I am doing is God's will. I think He has a plan for me. I'm part of something bigger."

You can talk with Sal Solo about his days with Classix Nouveaux. He may speak of the group's chart hits. And then there is the period beyond, when he went solo, and had several successes, particularly "San Damiano" ("Heart and Soul"). But I feel it is all irrelevant to him now, although he is aware that some time someone may plunder that old catalogue, and the group will be back in favour.

His past has given him a wide knowledge and awareness of all aspects of music, from writing and arrangement to overall production and performance. So his focal point these days comes down to the question, "How can I make my experience of real use and value to people?"

He is not hungry to make a foray into the recording arena for a hit song, although he would quite like to see something spiritually substantial in the national listings. He does keep very much in touch with what is happening in the current musical output, but only because he enjoys much of what he hears. and because it has the spin-off effect of enabling him to make better communication with people in the arena that matters most – the faith.

Sal Solo is outwardly a gentle person, articulate, intelligent and bursting with ideas. His gentleness comes from a deeply-held and practised faith.

Those other attributes come from his very nature, and have their springboard in his total dedication to the things of God. I remember this commitment from another meeting with him that took place five years ago when, in the journal *New Christian Music,* I quoted him saying, "To me my faith is all of my life. It means everything to me. I believe what I am doing is God's will. I think he has a plan for me. I'm part of something bigger. To me, I'm responding to God by laying my musical career on the line. Some people want a different vocabulary or they want one form of speech for general times and then another elsewhere. I don't understand this segregation. You don't have to announce it, just be it."

The commitiment remains the same. The intensity remains. It's just that now he's seen so many things happen, and he can say God was there. Because of this he dislikes the second rate, the slovenly, the ill-prepared approach to God, and its execution. For, surely rightly, he wonders how God can be glorified if we take little care and serve up not even the second best.

We met at Sal's very individualistic flat in northwest London, the outside unprepossessing, but inside a treasure trove of character, including the reminder that Sal is an accomplished artist, for that was the direction he first took before the demands of his music career.

In somewhat fading light, only latterly brightened by a small table lamp, he talked much about his sense of call.

You soon discover that Sal does not "do" because he feels like it, because it may be useful or demanded by a particular Christian community. He believes that God has called him to be where he is now. Throughout his musical career he has brought together countless groups of people, has planned modern worship, posed basic religious questions to people of all ages. Like most he has met opposition and misunderstanding, but he ploughs on, talking and singing of faith. When he first spanned the Roman Catholic-Protestant Evangelical boundaries he met with some harsh responses. In that article written around 1985 (the magazine has no date) he had commented on the narrow-mindedness and open hostility of some people at the Greenbelt Festival. Some of them would not pray with him, or say the Lord's Prayer. It astonished and hurt him. But most of that has gone, he has crossed the dividing lines, and the very authenticity of his strong beliefs has endeared him to many. Now, he regularly either sings or DJ's at the August Bank Holiday Greenbelt. By the end of 1990 his general radio DJ activity had declined.

Success in wordly terms has ceased to attract him. He doesn't have particular memories of a pop past that he would wish for now.

"I suppose I do think back sometimes, but mainly when someone seems to lead the conversation that way. Yet it doesn't really interest me that much. The 'life' I want is now. It is the looking for new opportunities. To try and read God's will is not easy but I must in prayer and devotions ask 'What has God set out for me?' Yes, I do have professional knowledge of the communication field but that is not the point. The real thing for any Christian is seeking 'that' will."

Here, he takes us all into the demands of the Gospel, in terms of belief and living. He has little sympathy with those who give out a faith that entertains and seems trendy but in reality offers little of God, hardly a real challenge, and is in a way merely aping an emotional process that is allied to the emptiness of the pop world.

His happiness comes from being consulted and asked for advice, from knowing that people feel he can offer something distinctive and substantial. "I mean, in pop, who remembers me? What I did was expendable. There is nothing particularly significant.'' Perhaps people will forget his Christian contribution, but the effect will be passed on. But he is aware there is a sin of pride. That it is difficult to dissociate the personal from what is offered.

Sal is not one to say that faith is instant, that it doesn't need time, and lots of time, years and years. ''As a person now, I feel much better able to come out with what I want to present. I see all I do as one part of the same whole.''

I remember from those years that he expressed appreciation of the way one-time Kajagoogoo musician Nick Beggs widened his religious thought parameters. He still feels gratitude. Basically Nick taught Sal that Christians of all shades and kinds can relate, can come together. Also he learnt that witness and work can have a wholeness. He sees his role at times as listening. ''People sometimes knock on the door and they want to get things clear. And I just sit and take it in. And my contribution may be very modest. I may be in a caring process. Sometimes it's a case of helping.''

His aim in his predominantly ''Christian'' youth work is establishing the centrality of faith to all things. He hates the divisions people make between the ''material'' world (non-church affairs) and the ''religious''. He is distressed when even ministers of religion cause these barriers. Sal is a Roman Catholic, and is sometimes staggered by how people see a religious duty in attending mass, the minimum bottom line of parish or distinctly Christian obligation, and then anything goes.

Yet this one-time much-discussed pop star is hopeful. He has seen too much happening at a basic level for him to wallow in negativity. God has kept his word for Sal.

19

ADRIAN SNELL

"If I Were"

"I am keen on finding new things, new ways of expressing the faith."

"If I Were" is a song from Adrian's album, *Father*. It seems the right title to describe the conversation we had one early December evening.

Our talk centred on a little-discussed and under appreciated area of the artist's life – the perpetual "being away" from loved ones.

Once upon a time we met fairly often and had regular conversations and appraisals, but the last five years or so have seen no meetings between us. Both of us have been very busy, and there have been important happenings in our lives, not the least the deaths of our fathers.

Dominating much of Adrian's thinking of the past few years, outside of his wife and three children, has been the death of his father, Geoffrey Stuart Snell, former Bishop of Croydon and of H.M. Forces. His death was a shock. He was not expected to die, for he had gone into hospital for a by-pass operation, and it was assumed he would come through the ordeal.

"It was a most distressing experience that lasted two weeks. And since then I've needed so much time to work it through. He was very special to me. I felt he understood me so well."

Arian is not suggesting that their relationship was one of perpetual calm, free from the misunderstandings that invade the relationships of most people. "Simply, there were so many things we could talk over. Call it trust. I was fortunate. I don't think I could have asked for more. He knew my failures and conflicts. The thing was this – we were never together enough."

It is probable that most people feel they could have done and said more with and to someone who has died. But for Adrian, as with all artists who have snatched a modicum of success that takes them away on the road sometimes for months on end, the very nature of their calling intensifies this separation. Yes, there is the joy, in his case, of working for the Lord, but there is much personal loss.

Adrian's sense of never spending enough time with his father carries over to his relationship with his wife, Sue, and the three children aged three, five and ten. Because of his work as an artist he spends an inordinate amount of time missing those little things that make the family so special.

He knows how some other people have reacted: they have pushed away their "calling", or they have watered down their intent to an almost unrecognizable degree. He admits he could have founded a musical school of sorts, run courses, tutored in the writing of religious musicals, and so forth. However, he feels that he must be himself, and that is an artist, a performer, not a teacher. This is his calling and commitment. "This is what's in me. This is where I believe God wants me to be. I do think of alternatives from time to time. But I still have a buzz. I am keen on finding new things, new ways of expressing the faith. I am still searching for new audiences, new areas, to widen the appeal, and I think over the years this has happened."

All this talk of dedication, and offering of himself to the Lord as a vehicle through which the Spirit can speak, is no smoke-screen to hide the cold blasts of reality. Telling me some more about his personal reaction to just being an artist, and the effect it can have on precious personal relationships, he continued in this vein.

"When you're on the road for days, sometimes weeks, well, you have time to think, and sometimes it's not the wisest thing. And you miss those you love, and you know what they are doing, and you would love to be there. And I miss them a lot.

"It's hard to explain to those whose lifestyle does not consist of endless coming and going. You can be home, and it seems that all too soon you're off again."

He tells how some people write and tell his wife how good she is for letting him be away and help them. "They say 'Thanks for letting him come', but I'm sure Sue says sometimes, 'I haven't let him go – he's just gone,' and these writers 'haven't asked me.' She has a lot to deal with, and I guess she has accepted things, but there is a lack of choice for her." And there *is* a price to be paid by his wife so that he can continue his God-given work.

Adrian's children have known nothing else. Their dad is with them, and then he leaves, but he returns. He feels that they understand, in so far as they can, at their ages. He misses many precious moments in their upbringing. "I remember the time Jamie was going for his gold in swimming. And I had watched him progress, but when the time came for his final process of 'doing for his badge' I was in Norway. I felt the loss. I rang but it's not the same thing, and there wasn't even a video."

So, it requires a very strong personal faith from both Adrian and Sue, and a quality of absolute certainty in the understanding that this is God's will. But they have been deciding on some very basic measures to counteract this loss of time together.

Tours will become shorter, where possible, and of two rather than three weeks' length in Britain and other European countries. On a special calendar, birthdays, anniversaries, and other family occasions have been clearly marked, with the idea of avoiding dates that clash, and ensuring that Adrian is at home to share in these family *big* days.

"I'm getting older, and 'precious' moments recede all the time. I mean you cannot recover a missed birthday, and my kids are always developing, and when you have someone who is ten then very soon there will be major changes, as he moves quickly from being a boy to a young man."

And he wants more "shared" moments with Sue, and together with the children. "Sue has been very realistic about everything. We have lost a lot of each other with all my travels. And it can be costly. Yes, there are dangers in any relationship when there are times apart. And even at home, I have to watch things, for I can be in the state of 'half-in and half-out', my mind wandering on to new musical ideas and projects, for it's when I'm off the road that I can do some thinking about future musical projects."

He uses the word "selfishness", and says it is easy for an artist to become self-thinking and absorbed in what is exciting, and forgetful of others who are not always "in tune" with this. He tells how he can become obsessed with what he is doing, and respond, even when "off" the road, to the perpetual activity. After all, even when he is not touring he can find himself for days on end in the recording studio, closed away from the world even more than when he is fulfilling a touring schedule.

"In what I do there must be a degree of self-promotion. Some people might think it is a matter of just going out and singing. But we have umpteen important sidelines, not least the time taken to move from one place to another, the setting up and testing of sound systems and musical equipment, meeting people, interviews . . . and the list can go on.''

He spoke of how "my faith has become much more mature. I've been especially thrilled with going back and exploring the essential Jewishness of Jesus. I think so much has been lost by people not enquiring and learning from this dimension. I think people have not made God big enough.''

He has been trying to resurrect much of the early "feast" schedule of the first Christian communities and of course taking that back into the time of Jesus and even earlier. "I get very disturbed when I encounter anti-Jewish feeling. It is not right.''

His excitement extends into the political arena, "to see the freedom that has come in many parts of the Eastern bloc, and the hunger I've encountered there for spiritual things.''

And more than anything else he praises God for his goodness and care through all the upheavals that are demanded from the artist, and are rarely appreciated by others. He feels he is so blessed by his family who miraculously keep with him. "I couldn't ask for more. I have been so fortunate. As I get older I think I am listening to others more! Sue says I don't let go enough. And I know that because of what I am doing, her own choice is restricted. There is always a price to be paid for most things, that is one seemingly certain aspect of life. Negatives must never rule the day, and that is why it is important that we should focus on God's love.''

20

STRYPHER

The thundering sons

"We've stood up for Christ. And we've taken a lot of heat for it. We've taken verbal abuse and been made fun of, but we've done it."

American band Strypher have declared war on Satan, and they do so in an area where to some degree Satanism and occult worship receive notice.

Group member Oz says, "At one time there were a lot of bands going Satanic – Motley Crue were getting the pentagrams out. We felt that the only way to be any kind of example against anything that's bad was to be with God, to be with Christ. He would be the only way we could keep strong."

Strypher shout, "We are the thundering sons" in the arena of hard rock rather than metal, but there is an affinity, and often a shared audience. "White" Christian-inspired metal, as opposed to occult-ridden "black" metal has spawned countless bands and recordings, with leading US Christian music journal *Contemporary Christian Music* often giving it separate space from other musics. But when it comes to making a sustained impact outside of the religious world, then Strypher have been "the" band, with their music attracting general chart fortune in the United States.

Strypher have been given much praise by the general hard rock – metal press, but their motives have been questioned by some writers, while considerable distaste has come from some conventional Christian quarters.

People have asked if they have used their religious image as a publicity stunt, or as a short cut to general fame. Britain's high-selling weekly *Kerrang* has headlined "Are Strypher the genuine article or is this Christian rock band, peace, love and understanding stuff just so much holy smoke?"

The *Kerrang* writer, Howard Johnson, was convinced that this indeed is the *real thing*. Johnson exercised an objective stance, but the group has not always received such commendatory treatment. Time and time again their very existence has been threatened by whisperings and innuendo. And, sadly some Christians have often been all too ready to accept the worst. And the slightest deviation from the presumed straight and narrow can attract a virulent spate of accusatory words.

During 1990, Strypher faced an onslaught from America's leading music culture journal, *Rolling Stone*. The boys were accused of deserting their principles, practices and beliefs. They were described as being tired of gibes, and were now drinking and smoking for all and sundry to see, and were fast changing their established principles.

The band denied the charges but admitted that they were being worn down by all kinds of people who were watching their behaviour, and that this was exercising an oppressive need for caution with regard to their lifestyle.

They confessed to being "burnt out" defending themselves against these spurious challenges. They spoke of how people always assumed the worst, with member Robert Sweet saying, "If they see me take a couple of girls in the bus then they think the worst thing, if they see me with guys they figure I'm queer." He adds, "As a band we say if you are for Strypher, then thank you. We hope we can put out music that people love, but we can't live up to people's standards. Nobody can. Everybody needs to keep their act together with God.''

So it is that Strypher see themselves quite simply as ''rock'n'roll evangelists'' – the ''metal missionaries''; a band that doesn't throw drumsticks into the audience, and instead dispenses imitation leather copies of the New Testament. ''Our message is J-E-S-U-S.''

Oz Fox says, ''Yeah, I do see what we're doing as a crusade.'' The band receive fanmail from all over the world, only most of what they receive differs drastically from the usual mail that finds its way to music stars. ''People ask, 'How can I be a Christian? What is it to be a Christian? I am a Christian, how can I become stronger?' '' Strypher members talk with zeal, with an awareness that they are venturing with the faith into an area where God-voices are thin on the ground. Theirs is not the territory of plain good old-fashioned chart hit music. Oz says, ''All I know is one thing: I'm here to bring the message of Christ to the world, and Christ has called me to do it. I believe in that wholeheartedly.''

Other criticisms that came their way as the decade opened would be quite familiar to Jesus music and ''Christian'' artists, namely that their song lyrics were becoming more generalized and less overtly Christian. In Strypher's case it centred on their album *Against The Law*. To some people they were not presenting ''Christ: Loud 'n' Clear'', as was the norm in previous times. Robert expounded on a ''sound'' difference, ''a little heavier'', and said the deletion of the words ''God'' and ''Christ'' was intentional, not because they were tired of the faith, rather it was part of a wider attempt to reach the mass-market audience. They felt some of their earlier work had not been playlisted by radio stations because it sounded too overtly religious, and some stations had Christians complaining that the message came clothed in a hard rock metal form. Said the artist, "If you don't get the platform, you can't make the statements."

Part of Styrpher's appeal has undeniably been to young Christians who have a rock-influenced background, and who, often, have to counter certain cultural rigidities within the home setting. Indeed, band members know this scenario for themselves.

Both Robert and Michael, the two Sweet brothers in the group, rebelled against their "born again" parents. The same was true for Oz. At one time the three ran a band that bore the name Roxx Regime. It seems that a Christian friend of theirs kept telling them that they should make music dedicated to the glory of God. On one eventful day the message struck home, the boys fell on their knees, prayed, and made their life-music commitment.

The trio, with Tim Gaines, were to emerge as Strypher, the name being derived from Isaiah 53: "And with his stripes we are healed."

Oz, speaking of the rather wild times as Roxx Regime, says, "I started to rebel because there were a lot of things her (his mother's) church was telling me to do that I couldn't. Like Robert and Michael, I knew Christ but didn't follow him."

Robert has said, "I became a Christian at fifteen after watching a lot of evangelists on TV and reading a lot of the Bible, but by the time I got to nineteen I was slipping away from it. The band was doing well, I was having a fun time, and it was easy for me not to focus too much on Christ. In the hustle and bustle of the day I started to forget the meaning and the purpose behind what I was doing. But when I started putting Christ second, the band started going downhill."

But now they are very much the thundering sons, with a determination to make the presence of Christ felt in areas long misunderstood or ignored by more conventional Christians. Are they angels from heaven or demons from hell? They answer, "Neither. We're people. We've stood up for Christ. And we've taken a lot of heat for it. We've taken verbal abuse and been made fun of, but we've done it."

21

DONNA SUMMER

Embracing destiny one day at a time

"All of a sudden this heavy weight that had been suppressing me for years finally lifted. I felt like somebody took tons off me. The anger and oppression of a diseased spirit was gone! I felt like a new person and like my whole life was ahead of me. I didn't feel that empty, sick feeling any more. I felt that God gave me a reason to be here."

Talking faith comes easily for Donna Summer, for it's her inspiration, yet she doesn't labour things. Possessed of assurance and friendliness, a stunning physical beauty and presence, Donna says, "I feel the divine presence upon me, my voice, my body, everywhere." In her lyric for the song "Voices Cryin' Out", from the album *All Systems Go*, she writes "the case of embracing destiny one day at a time."

All this is a great contrast from times and moments in her life when it seemed that the Lord was far, far away. She was a heavy drug user by the time she was into her late teens. She was part of a rock group at high school, and what she did was little different from the experiences of many kids in her neighbourhood. And when she left the United States to seek show business fame in Germany, and eventually found herself the new pop star of the world's record charts, the initial praise that came her way was not in honour of her vocal prowess but more for her sexual appeal. A journalist on *Rolling Stone* described her as a "servile vixen with a whispery voice".

This was so different from her conservative, Christian home background. Born LaDonna Gaines on 31 December 1948, in Boston, Mass., she was one of seven children of a Boston tradesman and a schoolteacher mum. LaDonna Andrea Gaines grew up with self-respect, and a sureness that the right things could be found in the Bible, church, and pre-eminently in Jesus. Here were the true realities, and thankfully, even if later she would forge through pretty heavy territory, the background remained in place; it was there to be called on.

Because Donna came from a church-going family, much of the first music she heard, and the sounds that gripped her, came from artists with a Gospel pedigree – the likes of Mahalia Jackson and Dinah Washington. But later she also developed an ear for rock, especially when the vocalist was Janis Joplin.

"I grew up in a family with five other girls and one boy, and we lived in a three-family house, so I had to compete. To be heard, you had to talk loud. Either that or you just tried to find a hollow corner where you could sit and fantasize about being someplace else. And school wasn't any easier. I went to school with some pretty violent people, and I was an outsider because I couldn't live on that black-and-white separatist premise. Racial? I didn't know what the word meant until I was older."

As for many black people, singing became the way of showing worth but for some reason her church choir director seemed unwilling that she should sing solo. And it made her angry beyond words. "Because when I screamed, I screamed loud," is her somewhat cryptic comment. It made her miss church, preferring the bedroom where she could play Mahalia records, practice her voice, and realize from an early age the importance of correct breathing.

Soon would come her venture into the general music world, the club scene, the drugs, the disorientation, the personal uncertainty. But eventually Donna pulled herself out of the tawdry self-destructive scene of which she had become a part, and she auditioned for *Hair*, a popular musical of the Sixties, and one that spawned much of the sexual and moral freedom of the time. It delved into the planetary system for thoughts of a new age, and was hailed in some quarters as a totally new, refreshing experience; for others it was no more than wanton permissiveness of a valueless kind. Her audition was successful, and she was invited to tour with the *Hair* cast, joining them in Munich, Germany.

Munich was a useful place for any aspiring singer and musician. Many well-known British and American acts and groups recorded in the city, and with English being the dominant language of much general European recording, there was a constant need for voices to help out on records being made by major stars. Donna had a voice, and most certainly, as photographs show, she was a striking personality.

Her vocal talent was clearly evidenced in the fact that once *Hair* had ended its run, she stayed on, not merely to find general studio work but so that she could join the Vienna Folk Opera. This move led her to meet an Austrian member of the cast, Helmut Sommer, whom she married, although they would later part. Later, a vowel change to that surname provided her with a useful name with which to embark on a recording career. She also starred in a number of German stage versions of popular musicals.

She would later claim that much of what she found and saw had little in common with Christian expression, but she was young, and one part of being youthful is a desire for experimentation. And sometimes there is unawareness of what is actually happening. A few years ago, she said, "I was recently thinking about the past, about some of the things I've done in my life and I cringe at the thought . . . At the time, they didn't seem at all terrible to me. But some of them were just terrible things. Like in *Hair* we would sing this song called 'Me and Lucifer, Lucifer and Me.' Think about that – me and the devil! When you're young you don't understand the implications. The devils's deception is so massive."

She met Giorgio Moroder and Pete Bellote, who ran the influential Oasis label. Both were fans of her vocal ability and general act, and they saw her potential for the future. It was for them that she would record the title "Love to Love you Baby" which was to become a massive worldwide hit. It was due to this that the once church-going Donna gained her title of "sex-goddess", emphasising the difference that had come into her life. Obviously, she was far from the girl of her youth.

Apart from a few of the hitches that hit most stars who have lasted the passage of time, she would now forge ahead, though at some cost to her personal happiness. "I found a hole in the market. I found a loophole, and that's how I got my foot in the door. I'll tell you that – not your basic, ordinary foot. And it boosted me up a long, long way from my Boston roots."

Such was her impact and the plethora of hits that followed almost instantly in its wake, that she was given to describing herself as a pop Marie Antoinette or Joan of Arc, "great women of their time who had to deal with ridicule and misunderstanding". Yet it might be said that she was surely not unaware of the way in which the pop-biz market can sell an individual as a product – and more, that once the word "sex" is allowed to rear its head, then the basic and earthy can soon devalue something precious and intimate.

Her rapid rise to fame almost led her into a nervous breakdown. She developed a chronic ulcer, found her new "star" identity difficult to live with, and occasionally spent a week at a time in hospital. She has admitted that her greatest fear was of losing control of herself, mentally and emotionally.

America greeted her homecoming after eight years with screams and record purchases. And in Britain she found a particularly fertile music market for her wares, especially since record contractual arrangements meant that her material was available from two different record groups.

So, she had success, of a kind that even the ambitious teenager of previous years could hardly have expected. But in the thick of her triumphs, and of monetary gain, with the music world at her feet, there was something amiss.

"I became very unhappy and felt empty all the time. There was a house, a beautiful child, a beautiful man. What was I missing?" Looking back to those days at one of our meetings, she told me, "It was a lonely time of my life, although I was surrounded by people." And what happened was almost inevitable − "I was into some serious, heavy drugs for manic depression. I was very suicidal, and without drugs at that point I probably wouldn't be here today. I was taking medicine for stuff that I should have been praying about. They were guilt patterns that I should have been asking God to forgive me for." At base Donna desired that she should be loved and understood: "I kept asking myself, why am I doing this?" She knew deep down that there were so many temptations that were overtaking her that she would forget who she was. "I think all human beings are insecure. Somehow we don't feel we belong here."

And then, as many people have done for countless generations, she just reached out and lying on her bed she put her hands upwards and said, "God, what do you want from me? Are you caring about me?"

In 1979, her sister brought a local pastor to the house and, quite oblivious of her early Christian connections, he began speaking of Jesus. She looked at him, and said, "Yeah, I know." The two prayed. "All of a sudden this heavy weight that had been suppressing me for years finally lifted. I felt like somebody took tons off me. The anger and oppression of a diseased spirit was gone! I felt like a new person and like my whole life was ahead of me. I didn't feel that empty, sick feeling any more."

The new Donna claimed, "I feel that God gave me a reason to be here." In immediate terms it meant that she began to translate her revived and new faith into her record activities. Her personal commitment was clearly shown on albums such as *The Wanderer* and *She Works Hard for the Money*. The former title contained one of the most powerful statements of faith recorded, namely the song "I Told Jesus". The latter saw her work with the foremost producer Michael Omartian, himself a Christian believer. The album clearly showed that Donna's sultry temptress days were over − a new and mature artist had arrived.

Donna says, "I'm a Christian now, a new person." And on *She Works Hard for the Money* the influence is most evident in "Unconditional Love", a strong, pushing musical base to adorn lyrics based on Paul's 1 Corinthians 13, and a recording that ranks with another evocative interpretation of Paul's words by Canadian artist Joni Mitchell, titled "Love", and located on the album *Wild Things Run Fast*. And she would show the social side of her faith with "Voices Cryin' Out" on the album *All Systems Go*.

Donna says, "I feel things have come together." Standing there, as we said goodbye at London's Inn On The Park, I was aware of her inner peace. Indeed, she has returned home to her real roots – the faith.

And of herself and the music world she says, "Entertainers are in a powerful position to influence the world for good or for bad. It's up to us to do things that are good and give people hope. That's the way I want to use my music now."

A year after her healing experience she married her live-in lover, Bruce Sudano, who is also now a Christian. Their first daughter was called Brook Lynn. They went to live in Santa Barbara, California, and three years later they had another child, Amanda Grace.

The new, Christian Donna brought prayer into the central areas of her life, even down to praying before her shows. She said, "I'm very aware of the power of God and it is important to be in his favour."

Faith held, lost, found again.

That is the story of Donna Summer.

22

U2

Light in the distance

"There is a battle, as I see it, between good and evil, and I think you've got to find your place in that . . . when you're there — when you're there where you should be and you know it in your heart — that is when you're involved." Bono

Here is the band that is held in almost religious reverence by many young people, some of whom are Christians. At the forefront is the lead singer, the dynamic and exciting Bono. He is one of four guys who discovered music together, and with one, possibly two of the other three, possesses a Christian faith.

But Bono, in common with the older mega-star of rock, Bob Dylan, has, it seems, little contact with organized Christian bodies, whether mainstream or in one of the myriad house and charismatic bodies.

Yet some Christian writers and magazines will say for U2 that they are the most significant Christian artists in the world today.

Generally most U2 chroniclers with a religious bent will delve back into the group's early times. They were part of the Shalom community, prayed and read their Bibles, learnt something of "separatist" Christian teachings, and then had to reconcile this with the worldly nature of rock.

As it was they left the Shalom movement, with its fundamentalist-charismatic emphasis. They found other Christian support, and they began recording albums that soon singled them out from the rest.

Their music has affirmed human dignity. They have asked for a celebrative attitude. They have often made use of biblical allusion and reference, sometimes obviously so, as with the exciting rock run of Psalm 40, in the song entitled "40". But I do not think their scriptural awareness has the depth and profundity of Bob Dylan when he recorded two majestic albums, *John Wesley Harding* and *New Morning*.

In his book on U2, Eamon Dunphy talks of writers seeing them at one time as "Bible bashers", but this seems an exaggeration. Voices, yes, said this, yet surely they did not control the media response to these fine musicians from Dublin.

U2 have had few deep and penetrative features on their song catalogue, partly due to a certain fear in some media areas that they might find these guys deeply religious (and, for media, that would never do – it is too serious a thing), partly reflecting a strange, though understandable, interview embargo. Perhaps U2 would find their religious statements treated with incomprehension or misunderstanding, especially since the media like things in black and white and demand quick responses – though more words might clear a few things up.

Whatever their status, in whatever world they walk, no one can claim mega-stardom as an excuse not to be found with the Lord's people breaking bread, praying, and expounding the Scriptures. Undoubtedly, there will be tensions in trying to resolve the "mix" of stars and so-called "ordinary" worshipping mortals, not necessarily because the former may make demands, but because the latter may well suffocate. However, whatever the way, there needs to be a resolving here, as elsewhere with other stars who say they are believers.

I am more happy with U2's unwillingness to adorn

conventional religious stages, for why should they? They must decide where and when and how their faith shall be made known. The way of Cliff Richard has been plain, and enormous good has come from what he has done. He has been part of mainstream Christian expression and been a willing participant in the activities of society in general, and of the establishment. That has not been the path of Bono, The Edge or drummer Larry Mullen. U2 have lent their support to certain social and political concerns, to fight for greater clarity on Aids, and to supporting with concerts and monies the work of Amnesty International. All three causes would seem infinitely more sensible than sharing the platform with doubtless worthy divines. Also, Bono spent time serving on an Irish government committee on unemployment.

On a personal level, and especially that of Bono, their influence has had a distinct religious flavouring, and is much commended (see for example the interview in this book with Maire Ni Bhraonain of Clannad).

Of course I, like doubtless others, would say that I would not "stitch" the band up, if I got near them. We journalists are not interested in running celebrity froth, nor in throwing a sickly religious mantle around them. A few of us, who have spent a lifetime in and around the music scene, and are also professing Christians, have music as a love, and we are not interested in "using" them for the purposes of making them palatable for people who even find Cliff Richard making sounds that disturb their religious preciousness.

But at least there is material from early times that can relate to the title of this book – *Feel So Real*. For there was a time when the band spoke more freely, and were not always treated as oddities because they had a powerful life philosophy, or as *Rolling Stone* writer Christopher

Connelly once put it, "even to raise the issue, to suggest that a person who loves rock'n'roll can unashamedly find peace with God, as well, is a powerful statement."

Connelly was sympathetic. Bono has said, "Sadomasochism is not taboo in rock'n'roll. Spirituality is." And the writer perceived that as a strong statement about the American scene, when noted against the electronic evangelism, and the bone-headed anti-rock movement.

The *Rolling Stone* feature saw U2's strength going deeper than most rock'n'roll outfits. I saw an articulate band – one that could speak to alienated youth, and who could overcome the indifference to spiritual things. U2 were seen as flying against traditional modes and materialistic grapplings, even if they became rich. Connelly had a perceptive note when he suggested that U2 worked on the level of not so much how *might* we live our lives (what we can get away with), but how *ought* we to live our lives.

These indeed are "lofty" goals, with U2's response then, and since, both positive yet abounding in contradictions. At the same time of the *Stone* article, U2 had released *The Unforgettable Fire*, named after the horrors of Hiroshima and Nagasaki, and paintings drawn by some who survived the death or suffering. And there was a passion and fury in *Pride* ("In The Name Of Love") that was devoted to the admired Martin Luther King.

Bono talked of his family, his faith and his belief in what he is doing, as the signs of *feel so real*. And he was not frightened to say that he felt the band had a rare spirit pervading its activities, that "we have this light in the distance." It all ran on the level of a remark he had made some time previously that when he was eighteen, he sensed that he had sensuality and spirituality, even if he didn't always understand the blues form.

On another occasion Bono said, "People tend to tie U2 up in ribbons and bows, but even I don't understand all the ingredients. For a lot of people we're *either* a spiritual band, *or* a political band, *or* just a rock band, *or* a band of 'dem liddle people who give de world hope . . .' but the real truth about U2 lies in the complications."

Of such is real life; but in the fantasy land of much popular show-biz, people are not too keen on the idea, unless the complications arise from sexual doubts, and preferably forays into the furtive unknown.

In "reality" U2 never imagined they would be the leaders of a whole movement of guitar and optimism, and constantly it seems they have to step back and consider where they are, and what is expected of them. But Bono has always known the "power" of rock'n'roll "The power is that it stimulates you emotionally, as you follow the singer, and physically, as you dance, and are hit by the music, it also has a cleansing effect; it's a great release."

But even a band that wishes to make people feel real by affirmative material can come unstuck. During their early tours U2, and Bono in particular, wanted graphically to illustrate their opposition to nationalism, and war. Bono raised a white flag as a gesture against division and when he sang "Surrender" he was saying that no one should kill for any flag. His traditional foray into the audience directly in front of the stage ran into trouble, with the flag being torn to bits, and he was involved in defending himself against physical attacks.

Bono has said, "There is a battle, as I see it, between good and evil, and I think you've got to find your place in that. It may be on the factory floor, or it may be writing songs. When you're there – when you're there where you should be and you know it in your heart – *that* is when you're involved. It may be trite, looking back on it; you know, 'I can't change the world, but I can change a world in me.' "

Such sentiment picks up the thread of his early life experience, for "I saw some really talented people getting into drugs and dying," and there was the time when his mother died. That sad event did not make Bono twisted and bitter against life, it sent him off on a serious quest for religious faith.

23

DENIECE WILLIAMS

"So glad I know"

"I look back on my career in music and I see how God gave me my mainstream success to use for His glory and to spread His message to a wider audience."

In her late teens Deniece Williams turned her back on her beliefs. She had her time of rebellion. But through all this turmoil she found one thing very true: "God wouldn't let me get away."

These days Deniece Williams is highly regarded in soul, R & B and gospel music circles. In the general record world she has had numerous hits as a solo artist, and two others when duetting with fellow American, Johnny Mathis. Early in her career she sang with Stevie Wonder's back-up group Wonderlove, from support to the 1972 Rolling Stones tour, until Wonder's memorable *Songs In The Key Of Life* set. There was also vocal work with some other artists such as Minnie Ripperton and Roberta Flack. And more important, she encountered Maurice White, then producer of the marvellous Earth, Wind & Fire soul outfit. Through association with White and the group she met Philip Bailey, an ardent Christian, who in 1981 organized "Jesus At The Roxy", an event that drew together performers who believed that Jesus was the answer. The result of Bailey's influence and prayers was Deniece's public return to the things she knew so well. The turmoil was gone, her heart and mind were offered to her Lord.

Back in "teen time", Deniece had followed a familiar path: she was given freedom – for she went to university 800 miles away – and she wanted her own way. "I think my experience is pretty typical of a lot of kids that grow up in the church – we just feel there are so many restrictions, so many rules about what you can't do, that you don't get enough of what you can do."

She says graphically, "I felt this was my chance to hang out and have some fun." She felt she could throw off long-entrenched truths and principles that had come from her "strict religious upbringing" in Gary, Indiana. Somehow it didn't work out that way. The looseness of college morals did not attract, any more than later she would accept some of the excesses of pop – usually enshrined under the popular trio of sex, drugs and alcohol.

Eventually Philip Bailey helped to bring her home. Deniece's first album was produced by Maurice White, and because of this she toured as support to the might group. It meant she shared daily Bible study and prayer with the singer. She found Christ in her own way, with her own experience, and let him transform her. Before, it had always been the case of feeling that something was being foisted on her. Now it would be first-hand faith.

She insisted that each and every album for CBS – there have been eleven – would contain at least one direct religious song. For one extra-special highlight, I would choose "Healing" from the album *Hot On The Trail*.

As far as general recording and stardom is concerned, she was to emerge as someone foremost in her field. Apart from achieving hit singles and albums, she was to tour the world under her own steam, and not as support to a supposedly greater artist or group. She grew as an artist: "Many of my sessions were fun, and very exciting.

Working with producers of diversity and talent was a great career and educational experience for me.''

Yet she always hungered for at least one special gospel set. ''Ever since I was a little girl I had wanted to make an album entirely devoted to my faith. I guess I spent quite a few years gearing up!''

She talks of six years of prayer, of searching for the right vehicle in which to express this long-felt wish, and then finding the right time. At times it became almost a compulsion. There was the incessant nagging within her that she had to let the faith be delivered in clear and cogent terms. The first album to result from this appeared in the early summer 1986 and was titled *So Glad I know*.

''I also spent a great deal of time looking for the right record company,'' her eventual decision being Sparrow, an American contemporary religious company. ''I wanted to present the message of Christ through music that would be appealing, innovative and highly marketable.''

She did so through a variety of musical styles, and high musical quality. Also she had a line-up of musical accompanyists that would make many an artist envious.

Deniece could record general material for CBS Records, and then, in America, issue this religious set on her Gateway Music House label, as if saying, there are two worlds. After all, she had been opposed by her major label in her aim to issue a ''gospel'' set as part of her overall record contract, so if she was going to achieve something, then inevitably her entire ''gospel'' set must needs find a religious outlet.

Obviously, this could give rise to two careers, yet she saw this as only temporary, ''I thought there would be a coming together of both areas. I was not torn between both, it was the way it was.''

She also added, ''Though I had inspirational music on

each of my pop albums, I had always wanted to devote one special musical project entirely to the Lord, and now I have. There is a song in my heart that can only be sung to him.''

Now she has several gospel albums to her credit, and is respected throughout the whole musical field. The observer of all this might suggest that much of her "gospel" inspiration is lost because there is a tendency for the media to categorize instantly, and push the description "religious" to barely recognized extremes, but this is to look at things from a British rather than an American standpoint. In America, and indeed in parts of Europe, there are gospel radio stations and paid-for gospel air time

None of this really seemed important to Deniece. On one of the several occasions on which I have met her, she talked of reaching people with the Gospel, and she talked of her spiritual songs, stressing brotherly love, peace, caring and kindness.

She said musical boundaries were senseless, but I fancy she was really unaware of the make-up of the British communications system. "When I accepted my two Grammys for *So Glad To Know*, I was able to stand up on stage and thank the Lord for his blessings in front of millions of people." Yes, and in America.

Deniece was quite aware that she would meet opposition, even from the religious world where some believe that the Word should not be heard in the clothing of contemporary music. But overriding her attitude and approach has been this inner sense of being called, of utilizing her name and skills in a very pronounced way for the Lord. It goes back to the time when she knew the Lord would never let her go. "When I'm judged, one question God won't ask me is why I didn't get the message out to the audience that he gave me. I will never be accused of that. I know that God has me exactly where he wants me now.''

There is an obvious sureness and confidence. It leads her to say, ''I look back at my career in music and I see how God gave me my mainstream success to use for his glory and to spread his message to a wider audience.'' You know it is coming from the heart when Deniece sings, ''I sing because I'm happy! I sing because I'm free.''

She told me, ''I do want people to understand Christianity, and I want them to 'fully' understand. I think Christian artists must stand on their chosen platform, and tell people what Christianity is, what the Bible is.''

There is an obvious passion in the way she speaks and communicates, and not surprisingly it makes her recoil with some hurt when the critics come out to carp. But propelling all is, yes, this sense of God with her. ''I wouldn't want anyone to think things are easy. There are difficulties in communicating, there are blocks in the way, but he leads us through.''

Yes, Deniece is a testimony to the fact that God is with us.

24

MANY AND VARIED

Jesus is alive and well

This chapter is a pot-pourri of a whole range of artists with whom I have talked in the past few years. They have told me of their faith. To one degree or another their belief has a Christian base, but the awareness of orthodox faith varies considerably.

Van Morrison keeps to himself. My Irish connections tell me that he has recovered his Christian roots. Surely no one who knows his music can doubt the intrinsic spirituality of what he does. His intense performance, and the emotional nature of his recordings stand almost second to none in contemporary music. To hear his recent works, such as *Poetic Champions Compose* with his mix of Irish literature, love and religion, or the superb Celtic feel of *Irish Heartbeat*, is to be brought surely into the presence of the Creator.

It was his duetting with Cliff Richard on the track "Whenever God Shines His Light" (found on Van's album *Avalon Sunset*) that alerted many to the possibility that the singer who has ranged through various religions and philosophies, faiths and styles, had become more centred on Christian things. Also it made many more people aware of the splendours of his music, for it is doubtful if too many of Cliff's fans have a wide musical awareness of a man who, after leaving the group Them, produced a record catalogue that stretches back into the second half of the Sixties decade.

Will Downing is an American from New York, who first
came to prominence via producer Arthur Baker's Wally
Jump Junior & The Criminal Element Project. Downing's
professional career started at the age of sixteen, and he
has a formidable reputation amongst the jazz and soul
fraternity. Pop people became aware of his existence when
he wiped the dance floor with a pulsating version of the
John Coltrane jazz classic "A Love Supreme". Coltrane's
long jazz epic was dedicated to God, some would say the
most powerful statement in the spiritual realm from the
jazz tradition. At the same time it exists as a simple love
song. A love song offered up to the Almighty.

I met Downing at Island Records and found him full
of verve and activity. We talked of the record and of his
faith. He told me, "It's my tribute to God's goodness.
To God in creation. I've been involved in gospel and I
am someone who asks, 'Why shouldn't we sing his praises
where it matters?' "

He reflected how he, in common with many others, has
found it easy at times to slip away from faith, or at least
from being part of a Christian community. "Unlike some
people I thought belonging to a choir was a kind of
punishment. Yes, I had a church background, but I wasn't
active. After a while I was into baseball and basketball and
I was too tired on a Sunday for church-going. I guess I
have always enshrined Christian values in my thinking."

However, of late he has been delving back into those
roots and going forward once more with a renewed faith.
"Now, I realize more and more what God is, what He has
done. It is more important to cultivate a sincere attitude
to things, that I should have a firm faith. I'm the youngest
of four and I've gained inspiration from those older than
me. I've been inspired by many black artists who are
expressing their faith, like Deniece Williams. I think the

Gospel gives you a positive attitude to things. I have no qualms in offering people inspirational music. I shall respect the One who has given life."

Downing called "A Love Supreme" a "God song". And that was what John Coltrane's widow, Alice, called it, and this was the reason she prevented Will from re-recording the number. Eventually, however, he satisfied her that he was not a blasphemous musical interloper.

Craig and *Charlie Reid* are brothers, and they write and perform together as a duo, The Proclaimers. Initial local support in Edinburgh and Inverness broadened to an English audience with their television debut in 1987 following upon a first successful UK tour. Then came their first album *This is the Story*. Several records have made them household names, particularly "Letter to America", and, late in 1990, "King Of The Road", a song that once enjoyed success in the Sixties and which they recorded for the film *The Crossing*.

They've performed at Greenbelt and have a great respect for the organizers of this Christian music event: "No one sets on you, and the people are so good. It's made quite an impression upon us."

They explain that they believe in something higher. They remain unsure about the whole panoply of Christian belief yet through Greenbelt they have seen how lives are changed, and that they must take account of a spiritual element in living. "We were not very aware of the Festival until we got invited. And we were surprised by the genuineness of the people. We do have a definite aim of including somewhere in our music a broadly spiritual aspect."

I got the impression that they were wanting to explore some more.

Ruby Turner had long been enchanting audiences, especially in the Midlands, before she found the wider national stage. She collected exuberantly-written reviews, both for "live" concerts and recorded material. She might be categorized as a soul singer but she was right when she said to me that that really limits her. In common with many pop artists she felt she must be free to express whatever comes to her.

She came to Britain from Montego Bay on Jamaica's north coast at the age of nine, to join her mother in the Birmingham suburbs of Handsworth before moving to King's Heath. As a child she grew up on a diet of reggae and later the bluesy and jazz end of soul, but was particularly struck by the extraordinary output of early Sam Cooke and The Soul Stirrers – and then there was the magnificent Mahalia Jackson.

Ruby was to find the British top thirty for the first time with "If You're Ready" (Come go with me): the classical gospel number from America's outstanding Staple Singers. And in her first reviews in the national press she collected from the *Guardian* writer, Robin Denselow, the lines, "If it wasn't for her wicked grin, Ruby Turner could easily be mistaken for the leader of a gospel choir."

Smile or no "wicked" smile, she started by singing in church. It gave her now powerful and big voice its airing, and gave her a vocal dexterity and an innate sense of rhythm.

She tells me of her spiritual awareness, of the "words" she heard in church, of the power of black gospel singing, of music's power to enhance and offer something much deeper than mere musical and lyric lines.

In a way, it would seem that gospel contributes to what she terms "searching for the great songs in our lifetime", the numbers that really speak to the soul, and indeed in her "live" performance she has the gospel spirit and ability to reach beneath the layer of skin that most of us shield ourselves with from the icy blasts of encountering truth.

Linda Womack is one half of Womack & Womack, the other half being her husband *Cecil*. She once said, "You can go for so long on junk food, but in the end you want a good meal, It's the same with music. It's food for the emotions." I soon learnt, even if I already knew, that "food" for the Womacks centres very much on "gospel" sounds. Cecil recalls how his early music influences included such fabulous gospel outfits such as the Swan Silvertones, Spirit of Memphis, the Staple Singers and Aretha Franklin. One other name was brought forward by both – Sam Cooke. Hence the duo stress the power of love in their music.

In Atlanta helping the poor and down and out, you can find singer – songwriter guitarists *Amy Ray* and *Emily Saliers*, collectively known as Indigo Girls, who serve up musical fare with radiance.

Their eponomyous debut album contained several spiritual numbers, including "Closer to be True" and "Prince of Darkness". They say that nobody "can speak across the board except Martin Luther King Jnr., or Jesus Christ." They speak of their music drawn on biblical traditions, and if they do not emerge as card-carrying Christians, at least of a traditional kind, then it is none the less obvious that Jesus figures strongly in their overall thought and eventual social action. Some might feel uneasy with their statement that "If you're a Buddhist or a Jew or a Christian you can look at the songs and reaffirm what you believe within the realm of your faith. We try to transcend our own background.

Amy stressed the word "motivation" during our conversation. "We've got things to say, we play music because it's fun to do. It's a gift, a privilege. I think, though, that there is something responsible being an artist. We want to lift people's self-esteem, make people feel better, and make the world a better place."

She sees the two of them working toward making people see, and be aware of, the evils that exist, and to do something about them. Both of them, for instance, work with the down and out, when they are not on tour. "Some people would rather not know that racism is on their doorstep, or they wish to push away nuclear threats. But many are insecure. We're not blatantly political. We just want to make people realize what is happening out there."

They concern themselves with AIDS sufferers. "We have worked for a volunteer group in Atlanta, and we play some benefits to raise funds. We're concerned, yes, with specific programmes, but the real caring has its calling at ground level. We feel we must put something into the world, and support people who need strength. And I would claim that I am a Christian."

Scottish band *Runrig* have been a favourite band of the Greenbelt people, as they carry with their music something of Scotland's Gaelic tradition, and Christian values. They told me on one occasion, "Our songs have a life perspective, they deal with an element of justice, a presentation of values, that people hold dear. We are against manipulation of things, the few abusing the majority, power held by the wealthy." They talk of helping people celebrate life but within the group there is a difference in how far the Christian "thing" should be stressed.

So too in the Greenbelt bag is Liverpool band *River City*

People. They enjoy playing the Festival, respect the Christian beliefs upon which they were brought up, but outside of that, it's not that easy to tie them down. I have had several good discussions with the band but have never elicited any particular commitment from any of them, other that a generalized feeling that there is something worthwile in the Christian message.

The popular Glasgow band *Deacon Blue* has been well favoured by Greenbelters, and in the summer of 1990, with the band by then riding high on the British music scene, they triumphed at the Festival. Much of their Christian content has come through Ricky Ross. Ross, songwriter for the group, conveys atmosphere more than message. And with Andie Brodie, an ex-student of the Royal Scottish Academy of Music and Drama, also having a Christian background, they have brought Christian values into play.

The first year of this decade saw the emergence of a remarkable American girl singer, *Mariah Carey*. Her self-titled debut album showed well her five-octave breadth, and had an inherent spiritual quality. But much more "Christian" in a demonstrable fashion has always been the music of *Paul Johnson*, who was twice in the Eighties fêted as Best British Male Gospel Singer for his performances in the London Community Gospel Choir. He then ventured into solo pastures with material that was initially well received. He says, "Essentially my singing is about self-expression, a personal thing. The thing that always struck me about vocalists such as Aretha and Chaka was their willingness to go with whatever they felt a song needed. That's not something you can prepare for; it just hits and takes you to another place. Well, I know what they feel and I want to use it too." He accepts that his gospel background and grounding has given him the freedom to do just that. He names Andrae Crouch among those who have influenced him. "I know I have gospel within me. And from someone such as Andrae I learnt funky soul gospel, and that I could offer my work in various musical idioms to the Lord. I guess one of my major spiritual songs has been "Father, Father". It's a personal gospel song and it's to do with my own failings, what I need, and how I feel, and what I have to do." He talks of having a spiritual eagerness, and the fight not to fly away from what he knows he should be as a person.

Johnson is one of a number of black gospel-based artists who have broadened their appeal, and left behind them solid roots. "There are those who say I've left the church. Well, I say, I am now more aware. There is a commitment you make according to what you feel, and I made it. And I am not some kind of backslider."

Actor and singer *Paul Jones*, of Manfred Mann band and the Blues Band, is one example of how Jesus can change a man's life. Once he assailed Cliff Richard on television because of his faith. Now he is a convinced church-going Christian, and he has the added bonus of his life's partner, Fiona Hindley, the actress, as someone who ardently shares his faith.

His conversion story is quite unusual. He had a passion for the paintings of the eighteenth century German artist Caspar David Friedrich. He saw the artist's religious works as imparting a spirituality that compelled his attention. He had the same reaction when he viewed the artist's general works, and it struck him that religious faith seemed paramount at all levels of life for Friedrich.

Yet Paul was an atheist. He found it disturbing that he, a non-believer, should be attracted in this way. Suddenly, along with his wife, he tried church-going. They attended the Luis Palau mission in London, and when the appeal was made, Fiona went forward for counselling. Paul followed. Up until now they had been living together, and this changed, they married.

Since their conversion and dedication both have developed their Christian commitment through media work. Life is different and through God's grace they have brought the Gospel to many.

I knew *Ray Goudie* of Heartbeat was a Christian simply because the band came to the fore on the basis that they would tell the Gospel through the pop channel of communication. Less known is the story of Ray's own willingness to follow God's call when it came. In 1978 Ray was concerned that he was unsure of God's reality, and resolved to give up his Christian activities unless he received what he would know as the "Word". Unknown to him, his wife Nancy had been praying for him. He was at Spring Harvest, playing drums for the worship group when he heard Luis Palau give his testimony. He realized, "I didn't have a close friendship with God. I was telling other people to become Christians and not having any reality myself."

Later he was taking part in some Christian work in Canada. He read a book entitled *Elijah*, by F.B. Meyer. It had a profound impression upon him, and for the first time he believed he could ask God and receive.

He was approached by a stranger who suggested that the reason for his lack of real commitment was that God's call had been pushed aside in the practical swing of his life. For Ray, that was the family shoe business, and it had been assumed he would follow in his father's footsteps and maintain it. The big moment came. He obeyed what he believed was God's calling, even though he knew it would cause initial heartbreak for his parents who had continued the family business. When I met and talked with him, I was impressed by his manner, the more so because I have not been moved by Heartbeat's forays into the pop world, and he was gracious enough not to take exception to my lukewarm approach.

The *Sister Sledge* girls of Philadelphia say faith has kept them going through thick and thin. These hit-makers of such enchanting disco records as "Thinking of You", "He's the Greatest Dancer", "We are Family" and "Lost in Music", have a Methodist minister dad, while Grandma is a staunch Baptist. It seems the girls grew up attending both churches!

Kim tells me that "Prayer is everything, it was a great experience just finding that. We pray each day. We have our Bibles with us on tour. And we keep in contact with the church. Too often we're in a plane or whatever but that can't stop us reading our Bibles. You have to keep in contact with God!"

Gloria Gaynor is another name from soul circles whom I have met, and then become aware that there is a Christian spirit beating away in her body. Gloria captured many a heart, and purse, as the cash tills rang for her mighty hits such as the strident numbers "I Will Survive", "I am what I Am" and "Never Can Say Goodbye". One of my early meetings with Gloria, as indeed with the Sister Sledge girls is recalled in my book *Rock Solid*.

Natalie Cole is another who stopped me in my tracks with a passionate telling of her Christian belief. And then there is *Whitney Houston*, daughter of Cissy, brought up and reared on solid Christian ideas. She told the pop journal *Smash Hits* in 1990 that "There is a love when you know the Lord or God for yourself that no man or human spirit can fulfil. It's a spiritual thing. It's coming from God. Which goes far deeper that the human love for me."

And who can forget the songs of *Rose Royce*, with their great pop numbers such as "Car Wash", "Love Don't Live Here Anymore" and the much revived "Wishing on a Star". When "Car Wash" had another revival near the end of the Eighties, I remember having a talk with Gwen Guthrie, and finding that this lead singer of Rose Royce was very much in the Lord.

The roll call of singing greats with Christian conviction can continue! There is *Philip Bailey* of Earth, Wind & Fire, whose solo religious albums have been such powerful statements of personal faith. And particularly well known in Christian artist circles is the affable *Nick Beggs* who sprang to pop fame with Kajagoogoo, and who set out to confront satanic occultism, nihilism and the plain life-negating ways of some major pop stars. He says, plain and sure, "I think the most important thing in life is one's relationship with God."

As a young teenager *Helen Shapiro* almost provided Cliff Richard with some severe competition in the pop field. She emerged in the pre-Beatle years, and although her hit trail continued until 1964, the most successful singles came during 1961–2. Quite why she disappeared from the big-time remains one of the show-biz mysteries, although in itself it is unsurprising, for the story of pop is the story of stars who come and go, after collecting a handful of hits.

These days Helen is an accomplished jazz singer. The jazz club world lacks the razzmatazz of the pop scene; places and venues are few and far between unless an artist goes totally overboard, playing to the chicken-and-chips-in-a-basket audience that talks rather than listens. Hence, her skills are not commensurate with her deserved public acclaim.

She has toured with Humphrey Lyttleton and his band, and radiated class. She is Jewish, and I remember her reluctance at one time to say clearly and decisively that she had become a Christian convert. Understandably, she was a trifle wary of becoming a Christian media show-piece, and in any case her first concern was with the tensions within family and beyond at her acceptance of Jesus as the promised Messiah.

At the time I had interviewed her for a musical paper, and I promised then that I would not go overboard in an excess of journalistic zeal but would leave her, as is her right, with the task of quietly pursuing the new faith that she had chosen.

Times have changed. Gone is the embarrassment she one felt at going into a bookshop to buy a Revised Standard Version of the Bible. Among formative influences in her Christian acceptance was *Betrayed*, a book by Stan Telchin, in which the author traces the path of his own daughter, for she had found that the Messianic promises in the Old Testament had their fulfilment in Jesus. Also she gained enormous strength from the ministry of Bob and Penny Cranham. It was through their witness and prayer that she came to know Jesus, and was introduced to a Christian community. Now her mother, as well, has become a believer. Helen says, "I'd been searching for the meaning of life and the Messiah of Israel was knocking at my door all the time." Now she sings and witnesses to the new Person and power in her life.

For any person there may be acute discomfort in having to tell of a change in lifestyle, especially given a sensitive and withdrawn nature. And Helen is no exception as she, more than most, had the task of telling her story to a definite religious community. Pop people often feel ill-suited to tell their fans, and the pop world in general, that they have become Christians. In some quarters religious belief is regarded as a regressive action that has no career appeal. But for some artists it all seems a great deal easier, for they start with the advantge of being reared and raised in a religious environment.

Bebe and *CeCe Winan* can claim a great Christian home background. Their parents, David ("Skip") and Dolores Winan, are seen as loving, church-rooted parents. BeBe and CeCe grew up with church-going as a natural act, and they soon sang in church, and gained much experience for their later role as singers. Also useful in later years was the simple fact that their family spawned the now legendary Winans.

I met them for the first time at The Greenhouse in London. Word Records had arranged a press conference. It was unfortunate that it was a horrendous British winter's day with rain pouring down, which hampered them, for their flight into Heathrow was late. Yet for all the negative factors they exuded a freshness and verve that belied the wintry conditions. They talked of parental love and wisdom. They felt they had the right foundation to their lives, and that it was not so much "that they groomed us to become gospel performers. They simply supported and believed in us."

Obviously the duo could have become part of an extended Winans, or as they put it "the Winans Choir", but they chose their own way, and have won numerous gospel music awards, and BeBe has been part of a Broadway production, *Don't Get God Started*. "You can't put God in a box. The world is in turmoil. All around you there's bad news, and the Gospel means 'good news'. People need to know that with Christ there is always hope . . . even in seemingly hopeless situations.''

Although a great deal of their support is in the religious record-buying and concert-going world, the two do find extensive reaction in the general soul and R & B fields, and there they have not watered down the message or programme content. "With our music, we're saying, 'accept Him', for He can come in.''

Testimony from their brothers and sisters is equally strong. Carvin of The Winans will discourse on the pressures Christian artists face in following through the commands of Christ. Brother Marvin says, "as long as Jesus is the centre, then immediate danger should dissipate''. "We feel God has equipped us mentally to deal with it.'' They admit it has not been easy when they are regarded as the "first family" of gospel music, and people look to them for standards, while there are also those who mysteriously, and sickeningly, wait for their fall.

Ronald Winan says, "We've depended solely on God's direction and knowing for ourselves what He had slated for us to do. I'm thankful for the way God has brought us. Our ministry has been geared toward the secular world. Our ministry is in the highways and hedges.'' These days The Winans consist of four brothers, and they express considerable concern at what has been happening in black areas with countless young black urban teenagers being shot and killed. In the musical arena they are superb, recognized by the soul and R & B fraternity, with their records on the Quincy Jones, Qwest label, and distributed through the general record world by Warner Bros. They are very much in the forefront of quality black music.

But for contrast with The Winans, there is *T-Bone Burnett*, married with two children, and living in Texas. Arguably, he will never achieve the musical prominence of many artists and groups featured in this book, yet he is more talented than many known names, and his work with artists such as Leslie Phillips is extremely good. Burnett hates labels and shows little sympathy for those who hide behind the word "Christian" in the hope that a different set of standards might be applied to their work from ones that apply in the cold world of general music. He detests the simplicistic lyrics written by some artists. T-Bone believes it is wrong that people should assume the Christian way is an easy one. He finds it the most worthwhile, but everything is not a bed of roses. His clarion cry is for thinking Christians, especially amongst the music fraternity.

One of the most underrated music people is *Precious Wilson*, although she lacks nothing in determination. Precious graced the charts early in 1978 with the band Eruption, and soon became a favourite on the club and popular cabaret circuit. Yet once she left Eruption, things became more complex and difficult. In common with many an artist, somehow the wrong deals were made, a career hindered. Yet she has made some fine records, had a number of "almosts", backed some known artists, and among other things, she sang the title track of the film *Jewel Of The Nile*, which preceded the release of her first album that was titled after herself. She can be found Sunday by Sunday joining in the praise of a London church.

Generally it seems true that a division can be made between music people who are Christians, and those who are often called Jesus Music artists, and who are signed to religious labels, and seemingly appeal to the more "trendy" areas of religious sub-culture. The past few years however have seen a considerable interest from the general rock following in a number of so-called Jesus Music artists. The purveyors of hard rock, heavy and white metal have caught the ear first, and the eye later. Strypher have been covered elsewhere in this book, and in overall media terms can claim to be the best known. The list is extensive, and in common with the general hard rock – metal market, bands come and go, split and reform from the embers of several. This is an area that deserves its own more "music-based" book or encyclopedia, but at least one long-lasting name should be mentioned, on grounds of longevity and of commitment.

This is *Petra*. Their history stretches back to 1972, with early musical roots stemming from guitarist Joe Walsh, and the group Kansas. In the latter several became Christians and are now very much part of the harder-edged Jesus Music scene in America. Petra have attracted enormous crowds and can talk of selling in excess of 250,000 of certain of their albums. The band have attracted much praise from the general rock world, and have a "known" name, enough to warrant inclusion in some major hard rock metal encyclopedias. Their witness has never wavered, their testimony has never been compromised. In recent times the band has been campaigning against the sexual immorality, that they often see encouraged by certain media circles. Member Ronny Cates says, "We're not out to be some famous Christian rock band; we're not trying to be complex lyrically or bold musically; and we're not out after any awards or recognition. We just want to be a resource to the church and to be used by God in whatever way He sees fit." They despair that the church, in certain central areas, has run away from the very problems that interest youth. ''The churches have been so reluctant to deal with sex and to talk about sexuality, now it's gotten so bad that they're crying out for help.'' During 1990 the band had a close association with best-selling American author and Christian apologist Josh McDowell, and helped to bring their audience to his attention. McDowell majored on the data that whereas America in the mid-1980s had five known sexually transmitted diseases, three years ago, the number had risen to thirty-eight, and fifty-one by the decade's end. He revealed that one out of every seven teenagers is getting STD's, and more were born with an STD than were affected by the polio epidemic in the 1950s. McDowell's association with Petra saw countless young people come forward to what were called ''manipulation-free altar calls''.

But not everyone is happy with remaining in the religious music world. Certainly it is much harder to exist financially in Britain, and the outlets for testimony can be very narrow. For long seen as the leading British singer in the religious market, *Martyn Joseph* has been re-evaluating where he should be. Talking with Martyn via mobile telephone, as he wriggles his way into the corner area of a classroom, is possibly not the best environment or conducive to either brittle clarity or profundity. However Martyn is well on his way to broaden his musical appeal via a major record company concern.

"I see myself more and more as a singer-songwriter who is a Christian. I am not an evangelist in the narrow scope of that term. I am musically painting pictures and want all to see them. Where I am, outside of a few moments and times, it is very restrictive. And I do find many pressures at the moment, always being aware that someone is examining each and every thing I do. I want to say what I feel, and like, and am, much more.''

He talks of being the subject of thinly-veiled attacks, since much of his current material does not have such a direct religious language, and that leads some people to assume he is less Christian. "I am tired of misplaced prejudice and I've been hurt a lot. I would love the chance of battling it out on the general music stage."

Some aspects of his predicament are not new, for any person who creates material that reflects where they stand at a given time, must face the fact that this once very fresh work will be heard or read years later. By the time others become aware of the early thoughts and reflections the creator has moved on. "I think of some early recordings, and quite honestly I wince. I'm much more influenced by artists such as Bob Dylan and Bruce Springsteen than those recordings would suggest. I am dismayed that if I bring in the social gospel in my songs, some people react with so much prejudice. I do not want to be forever in a religious sub-culture."

In cold print, and indeed as I glance back, it might seem as though Martyn is either bellyaching or is being inordinately negative. But if you had heard his voice, then you would hopefully concur with my own impression that he was speaking honestly, and was doing so from within a positive context, namely that he has things to do and say, and he wants to say them. And he is doing so now as in the past, albeit in a more general music form, aware of his calling. He says, "I am not being true to anything if I wander somewhat ineffectually around a scene that needs new life." It is not the case that he is ungrateful for the help and guidance, prayer and support, that have come from some Christians. He would like to take them with him on the more perilous path of saying something to the great mass of people, where often even basic forms of acceptance can be lacking.

There are others, some of whom featured in my earlier book, *Rock Solid*. But what is one to make of those *enfants terribles*, *Madonna* and *Prince*, the two best-known names who make considerable use of religious imagery, and of their own religious backgrounds, yet whose image is an affront to many people.

Prince's chequered career, and somewhat bizarre antics, have been well chronicled, and can be found in such books as *Prince: Imp Of The Perverse* by Barney Hoskyns (Virgin), and *Prince: A Pop Life* by Dave Hill (Faber). Neither of these avoid the religious expressionism of the artist and this could hardly be otherwise considering the content of some of his albums. Here is someone who shouts at his audience that he wants them to love God, who signs autographs with "Love God" written clearly, who sings "Save me, Jesus" in the song "Anna Steisa", and told his listeners to "blow that devil away" in his song "No". He recites the Lord's Prayer between numbers, and for all intents and purposes he is more out front than a host of card-carrying Christian pop singers bar none, save perhaps Cliff Richard, and he is certainly more risqué.

But many would say he is muddled in his thinking. He is capable of electric religious thoughts, but his once bodyguard Chick Huntsbury put it delightfully when he uttered the unforgettable line, "Prince worships two gods – religion and sex. But he's confused over which one he likes best." There is nothing new in this when it comes to rock'n'roll, for many a star has wanted the advantages of faith to exist side by side with unbridled passion for anyone who comes their way. But with Prince, there is a move to almost defy what he does, either in his personal life, or out there on stage, where if he has a desire to clean up many a Christian's hang-up with the body as holy, it comes across in audience reaction as nothing more than soft porn. In reality he is an artist who blurs, and is all the more dangerous for it. It is not his analogy between sexual passion and religious ecstacy that is questioned, for that is something that might be said more often, for it's certainly a scriptural statement, even if it is ignored by many (read Song of Songs or Paul's picture of Christ and the church coming together with the union of bride and bridegroom). But there is no place in scriptural teaching for the view that sex is a higher form of consciousness than the overall path of spirituality. Nor is the sexual act seen as the total expression of ''sex'', and indeed with the fear of AIDS, many people have begun to realize rather late in the day, that you can be a sexual person in many ways. In the end Prince debases real good and true sexual being.

I am sure there will be many reading this book who will say that Prince and Madonna have no place in the pages of this book. Doubtless a good case can be advanced, but to write of people who ''feel so real'' because of their Christian convictions without at least touching on two major acts who throw religion at their audiences under the guise that it means something to them would seem as naive and selective as if someone wrote about the First Division of the football League and deleted Arsenal and Manchester United simply because both have been fined for bad game behaviour, and should therefore be ignored. I, a writer, am not in favour of bad gamesmanship.

Madonna is a more diffuse figure than Prince. The latter may sometimes wander into the fog of his own making, but at least there are those songs with direct religious comment, there are his stage performances, and he

sometimes utters religious statements. Madonna, of
course, does recite the rosary on the title track of her *Like
a Prayer* album, and at the time gained for herself from
a *Rolling Stone* interviewer the comment that it signalled
a post-thirty age philosophical nature, as well as portending
to be a personal spiritual purge.

There are comments: "When I was growing up, I was
religious, in a passionate, adolescent way. Jesus Christ was
like a movie star, my favourite idol of all." And conversely,
for all the adolescent phase, her home in Hollywood Hills
contains ever-present Catholic symbols of faith and
protection. She has described that faith as "dark, painful,
guilt-ridden" and claims it spurred her ever onwards into
being a flamboyant attention-getter. Her Catholic
education reinforced her feelings of being lonely and
unloved – her mother died when she was six, and for a
while she was shuttled from relative to relative, before
returning home to a succession of housekeepers, and then
her father's eventual remarriage. One of her ex-boyfriends
has said, "She's deeply terrified of herself and of being
alone with herself. Yet she's a more interesting person than
she knows, and a much more fragile person than she wants
to admit. But I fear for her if she doesn't change the way
she operates."

She has incited much bad feeling with her dress, song
lyrics, and accompanying promotional videos for her video
releases. She admits that she has incensed many, but
attempts to answer this by saying that children can sense
the "realness of somebody and the goodness of
somebody". But that fails to answer the basic question
of whether they should have to assess something sometimes
so sexual and unusual from their limited experience and
awareness.

"Feel so real?" Madonna? Who knows? Does she know?

One thing is sure. The sleaze and soft porn trade, including *Penthouse* and *Playboy* magazines, have not been slow to market her wares. And it has not passed unnoticed that if you dress a girl in underwear and have her act and sing in a sexually provocative manner, you have a better chance of a hit. And such is her skill at the quick one-liner comeback to questions, and an innate ability to tease, dressed in an often "send-up" stance, that it is never easy to know what she does feel. Ask her about normality and she will say, "Yeah. And I know it's gonna get weirder and weirder." And for a provocative one-liner, she will say, "I wanted to be a nun . . . then I discovered boys." Ask her about her name, and she will say, "How can I change my name? I have the most holy name a woman can have. But if I *had* to change my name, I'd use my confirmation name, Veronica. I chose her because she wiped the face of Jesus, which I thought was really dramatic."

"Feel so real?" Who can answer that question? Can she?

This chapter has included a wide range of personal expression, and its extent could have been increased if it had included a plethora of fringe-Christian material, as represented by artists like Peter Gabriel, Sting, Enya, Kate Bush and Paul Simon. What joins everyone together is a common respect for Jesus. That may not be enough for many Christians but at least it seems preferable to a virulent anti-Jesus voice. It would not be so easy to find a common feel for the Christian community, and even less so for the "Church", since outside traditional areas some people seem to equate their emotional negative regard for Christian things with the word "church", while allowing that there are some people called Christians who merit an audience.

It is quite clear from this list of artists, and those

elsewhere in this book, that the gloom of the John Blanchards of this world is unfounded. Jesus is alive and well, where He should be, in the lives of people and communities. There is positive witness. There is inspiring and deeply felt faith. And there is also a spirit of enquiry. People in the Arts Centre Group, those associated with Dave Berry's Servant Trust work, in the Greenbelt sphere of influence, can help in the overall task of celebrating Christ and at the same time bring people into an awareness of his significance.

END NOTE

As any writer and publisher knows, there comes a time when work must cease, even if some things remain outstanding. And I am conscious that I would have liked some more words with some of the artists I interviewed for my book *Rock Solid* of 1986 – but then not every artist with a "Christian" framework is available. And there are some names whose Christian faith has been made known since 1986 and whose story has still failed to make it here; I think especially of Steve from Lies Damned Lies, or, perhaps claiming less a definite Christian orientation, Ricky Ross and his wife Lorraine MacIntosh of Deacon Blue, and Peter Garrett of Midnight Oil. Next time folks?

But not everybody is at home, and so bear with me if someone precious to you has not made these pages. Who knows – a third book in the not too distant future?

And already, I have been talking with Amy Grant (top 5, USA Spring 1991) and King's X, who toured Europe, April 1991, with AC/DC, the hard rock mega-stars.